DADDY'S APPRENTICE

D0954786

DADDY'S APPRENTICE

Incest, Corruption, and Betrayal: A Survivor's Story

Sandy Wilson with S.L. Bolton

Writer's Showcase
presented by *Writer's Digest*
San Jose New York Lincoln Shanghai

Daddy's Apprentice
Incest, Corruption, and Betrayal: A Survivor's Story

Writer's Showcase
presented by *Writer's Digest*
an imprint of iUniverse.com, Inc.

For information address:
iUniverse.com, Inc.
620 North 48th Street, Suite 201
Lincoln, NE 68504-3467
www.iuniverse.com

Names of characters have been changed to protect the innocent.

ISBN: 0-595-13554-4

Printed in the United States of America

PREFACE

Dear Reader,

Evil feeds off the innocent. When evil has your father's face, it is devastating. This is my story, told as I remember it, first with the innocence and vulnerability of a child, then through adolescent eyes that began to question.

- S.W -

CHAPTER ONE

Northern California, 1965

In the walnut tree's upper branches, I crouch against the rough bark. My grandmother hugs me into her arms while my grandfather stumbles on the gritty grass below us. His flashlight glows in the night air spraying eerie designs across the backyard. Once in a while, a ray of light flashes outlining the glint of the shotgun barrel clutched beneath Papa's right arm.

"Mama, Sandy, come on out. I have a surprise for you."

My grandfather's cooing words rasp from too many smoked cigarettes and too much whiskey. I want to call to him, tell him, "Papa, up here."

Instead, I feel Mama's warm breath on my cheek as she gently shushes me and squeezes me closer. Even at four years old, I know the rules of the game.

On the nights when Papa's sickness takes hold, my grandmother warns me. "He's coming, Sandy. Let's go."

Because Mama has a special gift of knowing things, I scamper ahead through the backdoor to the base of the shadowy walnut tree. After scrambling up, I reach down for the plaid blanket. Then my grandmother grasps branch after branch with her strong, fleshy arms, lifting up and up, her painful groans traveling with her as her legs flail uselessly from fused hips.

Once settled in the branches, wedged between jagged tree bark and Mama's plump belly, I feel the blanket tighten around us, scratchy thread around bare legs. A smell of day old perspiration mingles with Mama's rose-scented toilet water.

"Keep quiet, baby. Don't move, you hear," Mama says.

Sure enough the backdoor bangs open and Papa comes to search for us. My heart turns over like the big bumpy wheels of a tractor. Through the tree leaves, glossy from the moon overhead, I watch Papa walking circles in the yard and around the corner of the house.

"Sandy, Mama, where are you? Come on out now. I have a surprise for you. Sandy. Mama."

What could the surprise be? Maybe Papa will take me and Mama to the dump tomorrow. We might get there after the candy factory truck leaves. I hope so. I like hunting through the heaping piles and finding rainbow candy treasure.

Shivering, cold from northern California's night air, I huddle closer to Mama, wanting to sleep, to go to bed. I wish the game was over, but like Mama says, if wishes wuz horses, we'd be rich.

I hear Papa step onto the back porch, his heavy boots scrape the wooden planks, and the screen door creaks then slams hard and loud. I shudder, my ears alert to the house sounds. Heavy footsteps from room to room. A light comes on in the back bedroom, thuds as Papa's boots hit the wooden floor.

When I lean forward, Mama whispers, "Not yet, little one. Not yet."

Papa's snoring will mean the game is almost over.

Mama tucks the blanket around me and lowers herself to the ground. Then her arms lift up, waiting to shield me from a clumsy fall.

We tiptoe around the far side of the house and to the front door. Mama leans forward listening. With a nod, she opens the door, we cross the dark, musty parlor, and sneak into the smaller bedroom.

Crawling between the layers of quilts, I curl next to Mama, nudging my head against her soft, warm back. She lies facing the door where a straight-backed chair is propped under the door knob.

"What's Papa's surprise, Mama?" I ask before settling down to sleep.

"Hush, baby. You know there's no surprise."

"Maybe this time…"

"Hush now, go to sleep."

I drift off lulled by Papa's hollow snores, the ticking of the white metal alarm clock, Mama's deep even breaths, and the possibility of rainbow candy.

When morning comes, I hear the low murmur of Papa and Mama talking in the kitchen. I smile knowing that Papa's sickness is gone for a few days and wondering if there is a surprise.

Later, I watch Mama clean the green coating off the bologna Papa brought her from his morning trip to the dump. Bacon grease sizzles in the black frying pan waiting for Mama to toss in a few slices.

"Ain't we blessed today, Sandy? Papa's feeling better and we got a good lunch cooking."

"Where's my surprise, Mama?"

"You shoulda knowed Papa was joshing. He had the sickness last night."

I blink back the tears.

"Hold on, now. Papa says he wants you to go up the hill after a while and sit on the bench with him. Your Papa spoils you rotten. He thinks the sun rises 'cause of you."

I tighten the sides of my lips trying not to smile. Mama says I'm prideful at times. Too big for my britches.

When she sets the plate on the table, the edges of the meat are curling up. I pour ketchup down the center and roll the slice like a log.

"Your real momma's coming to visit soon," Mama says as she dips a slice of white bread into the frying pan grease, sops it up, and smacks her lips after she eats it down.

"She'll be surprised to see how you've growed."

I shrug, looking at the ketchup dripping off my fingers. Secretly, I wish my mother wouldn't visit. I never know what to call her so I don't call her anything. Not her name, Kristen. Not mother. Not anything.

After lunch, I look out across the field. Far in one direction is an empty shack and on the other side I can see the tin roof of a neighbor's trailer.

Up the big hill, I see Papa sitting on his tattered bench. It's a car's front seat that he tore out of a wrecked Ford he found at the dump. The bench is his resting and thinking place. If he waves at me, I know it's okay to go sit beside him. Finally, he raises his arm and I run like lightening.

My grandfather smells like Lava soap as he hugs me next to him. The bench seat rocks a bit as I snuggle up.

"Gotta anchor this thing down soon."

"Mama says so, too, before we all roll down the hill."

Papa laughs so hard. He starts coughing. His cough scares me sometimes. It sounds like a rickety pump handle.

"Can I, Papa?"

He nods and pulls the black plastic comb from his pant pocket. I crawl to the back of the seat, legs around his head and humped shoulders, then comb the white hair that circles above his ears. His bald spot glistens shiny pink in the afternoon sun.

It's a perfect day.

"Got all my rounds done early."

"Any treats, Papa?"

"Not a one. Maybe tomorrow."

Papa collects garbage from the farms and ranches around town. Sometimes, people leave us clothes or food on top of their trash. Once someone left a bright red sweater with pearl buttons. The sweater is too little now, but I keep the pretty buttons in an old cigar box Papa gave me for my treasures.

"Can we go to the dump tomorrow?"

"No, baby. Gotta make the rounds of the stores. Thursday is clean-out day at the supermarket. Might even find you a' orange, if we're lucky."

"Can I go?"

"We'll see, baby."

I comb the damp strands of his white hair and am happy. "We'll see" means yes.

The next morning, behind the grocery store, the dumpster is heaped high. Papa lifts me up to search around. It stinks like an old ice chest and I wrinkle my nose tight trying to close out the smell. Then I catch my bare foot on top of a wood crate and topple into a stack of cardboard boxes.

Papa calls up, seeing if I'm okay. I laugh, stand up, and wave down at him.

Flies buzz around some mooshy lettuce. I clutch some dented soup cans and toss them to Papa along with some not-too-black bananas. Then I jump into Papa's strong arms and he sets me on the hot asphalt. I shift back and forth fast from foot to foot in the alley while Papa fills his potato sack with some green vegetables.

He says, "Mama'll love these here beans. Sandy, you go on in there and ask the butcher for some dog bones."

I smile. It's Papa's and my secret. We don't have any dog. If we're lucky, the butcher will give us bones with extra meat. If not, Mama'll cook them with her vegetables. Grease rising to the top is mighty fine cookin', she says with her Missouri twang.

Papa stays in the alley and I go around the big store through the glass doors. I ding the bell at the meat counter.

"What can I do for you, little lady?" the man asks. His white coat is smeared brown.

"Dog bones, please, sir." I smile wide then lower my head like Papa taught me.

The grocery store man gives me a big plastic bag full of heavy bones and a pat on the head. It takes both arms to hold the bag against my front.

When I get outside, I see Papa's beat-up truck. The blue paint has been scratched off and one of the lights is yellow not white like most trucks.

"We going to another store?"

"Been there. Nothing. Someone poured Clorox on all the food. What a waste."

"Clorocks?"

"It's a kinda stuff that cleans dirt outta clothes. On other things, it chews it up. The food's ruined."

"Why?"

"To keep us poor people out of their garbage, I reckon."

Papa's real quiet all the way back to the house. When he unloads the truck, he says to Mama. "I'm going down the road a spell."

"Stay home tonight, Larry. I'll cook up some greens with them rib bones."

Papa doesn't answer, slams the door, and rides off in his truck. The gravel dust blows and I know that Papa's sickness is coming on him again. It'll be time for hide-and-seek soon.

CHAPTER TWO

"Can't you speed it up some?" Mama says to Papa. "I don't wanna miss visiting hours."

"That prison's a filthy place, Opal," he says. "Not fit for man or beast."

"He's my son, Larry. A mother should visit her son."

"He's not my son. Al's nothing but trouble. Hurtin' my Krissy that way."

"Hush up now, little pitchers…" Mama says.

Mama forgets that I'm pretty smart for six going on seven. Somehow I've always known that Kristen and Al, my real momma and daddy, are brother and sister and I've always known to keep family business to myself.

I hadn't figured out how my father had hurt my mother though except for making her have me. Which didn't make much sense since Mama said I was a blessing.

Going to the prison meant that Papa had to drive long hours from California to Salem, Oregon. He was in a grouchy mood before and after. He'd always get his sickness real bad when we'd get back home.

In the prison parking lot, I sit alone in the car's back seat, peeking over the half-lowered window to stare at the huge gray buildings. There's a tall tower with windows all around it. The men in the tower wear hats that hang over their foreheads. They turn their heads looking in different directions.

My heart thumps hard when they look toward the parking lot. I hunch down. I don't want them to send someone for me since kids aren't supposed to visit the prison.

The door handle is hot against my cheek. I'm so thirsty and I need to go pee. I wiggle around trying to forget.

Someone is walking past the gate. Maybe it's Mama and Papa. No, two women are laughing loud. The skinny one in the flowery blouse carries a picnic basket and the other lady is lugging a plastic cooler. When they climb into a big pick-up truck, I wish I had something cold from that cooler.

Trying to forget my dry mouth, I stare at the gray buildings. Mama says the men inside are kept in cages like animals. I don't hear any growls or roars like at the zoo. Maybe they tape the men's mouths. Maybe they chain them to the bars. I never want to go to prison.

On the drive away from the ugly cages and back to California, I curl up in the backseat. I like to hear the tires thumping on the road and watch the lights whiz by like fireflies.

I hear Mama say, "Al wants to come on home when he gets out. I don't want to hear nothing more about it."

"After what he did to Krissy, to you?"

"Whatcha mean to me? I won't listen to your evil, Larry, you hear me. Sandy's sleeping. Now let it be. Just let it be.'"

I drift into sleep knowing that my father will be coming home and wondering what he looks like. Maybe he'll bring me presents. He's been gone so long. I dream of ribbons and a fuzzy white cat.

The next day Papa's already gone to town before I wake up. Mama lets me eat Oreos for breakfast. A treat for being such a good traveler, she tells me.

I lick the white out of the middle and dunk the brown cookie halves in my milk. They get mushy and color the milk with brown speckles.

"Drink up now. We got chores," Mama says.

"Do I hafta?" The milk tastes yucky with the spots in it.

Mama nods and I gulp it fast so I won't feel the bumps go down.

My grandmother hands me the broom and I sweep the trash out the back door, onto the porch and over the side. The pile will grow bigger and bigger, a paper mountain. Papa collects garbage all over town, but never takes ours. It'll be left there when we move.

Mama rushes out the door and says, "Uh, oh. Hurry, Sandy. Papa's got the daytime sickness."

She grabs my hand, tosses the broom aside, and we walk fast across the back yard. There's no walnut tree to hide in because that house burned down. Now we live in another house. Instead of a sheltering tree, we skulk behind an abandoned camping trailer. I can hear Papa's truck sputter gravel in the driveway.

Mama and I stand flat against the outside of the trailer walls. The chipped paint tickles at my nose. I sneeze.

"Hush, girl. Hush."

Mama's eyes are wide and her chest is heaving quickly up and down. She clutches my hand tightly then raises her finger to her lips. I raise my finger to my lips, too, and then I hear Papa.

"Sandy, Mama. Papa's home. Come out. Come out."

Mama shakes her head at me. Her dark brown hair clings to her sweaty face. I can hear Papa's boots kicking the other side of the trailer. The metal clangs.

Mama edges along the side, gripping my hand tightly so that my fingers feel squished. When Mama tugs me, my hair catches on the rough trailer wall.

"Ow!" I cry out. Mama grabs me to her as Papa rounds the corner.

"Down to the house," he says. His shotgun is pointing at us.

Mama walks as fast as she can down the hill. My feet are barely touching the ground. My arm feels like it is coming out from my shoulder.

"Slow down, old girl," Papa says. His voice is soft like an early fall breeze.

"Yeah, Mama, slow down. You're hurting me."

When we're in the house, Mama starts crying.

"Larry, don't hurt the child. Please."

I look from Mama to Papa. His face is red like the label of a soup can. His eyes are scrunched up.

"I do what I please. I'm the man in this house."

"I know you are, Larry. Let Sandy go out and play so's we can talk."

The shotgun weaves back and forth when Papa loses his balance. He grabs the edge of the kitchen table and leans on it to steady himself. Then he raises the gun again and points it at Mama.

"Al can't come back here again…never…'cause we aint' gonna be here."

Papa laughs funny-like. Maybe, it's just part of the game. No, Mama's shaking and trying to push me behind her.

"Hold on, Larry. You're right. I won't let Al come back here. I won't. I promise."

Papa's throat gurgles when he laughs again.

"You can't say no to Al, you never could, never will. Well, he can't have you or my Sandy. He can't bring his robbin', thievin' ways here. First, he got my Krissy pregnant, his own sister, then he takes her out thievin' Almost got her arrested. Wonder she wasn't in prison, too."

Papa sways a little trying to aim the shotgun barrel at Mama. I tighten my fists on her skirt and shut my eyes.

"Please, Larry. Don't hurt Sandy. She's just a baby."

"Ain't no other way."

I listen, but I can't look. Then, I hear a man's voice.

"Hey, Dad, you be target practicing in the house? Best put that gun down."

It's my Uncle Ely's voice through the opened front window. I peek around Mama's skirt and see him walking through the door.

"Dad, don't point the gun at Ma. It's dangerous."

"You're spoiling everything, son. Get on back home. Leave us be."

"No, I'm not leaving. Put the gun down," Uncle Ely says as he steps toward Papa.

Papa turns and points the gun at Ely. "This ain't none of your concern. Now get."

Uncle Ely keeps walking and grabs the shotgun barrel pushing it into the air. Then he wrenches it from Papa.

Papa grumbles something and shuffles off to his bedroom. Mama hugs me then Uncle Ely.

"It's okay, Sandy. It's Papa's sickness. He'll be just fine after some rest. You scoot outside. I wanna talk to your Uncle Ely now."

Both Mama and Ely slump onto the kitchen chairs. Mama buries her head in her hands and Uncle Ely puts his arm around her shoulder.

"You're a good son, Ely," Mama says. "He was gonna kill us this time."

"He's scared of Al coming home, Ma."

As I huddle behind the screen door, I hear Uncle Ely groan and say, "We all are."

CHAPTER THREE

A few days after Uncle Ely had kept Papa from shooting us and Mama had hidden Papa's shotgun, Mama was in a singing mood.

"You know, child. I been thinkin'. We ain't using that old camper back yonder. It'd make a mighty fine playhouse," Mama says to me.

"A playhouse? Really?"

"Yes, child, for your very own."

"Fine idea, Opal. Get your favorite toys, Sandy, and I'll help you carry them out back," Papa says.

Mama hands me a couple of paper bags for carrying my stuff. I load them up with dolls, plastic dishes, and crayons.

"While you're moving Sandy's toys, Larry. Go ahead and store up them boxes I've been packing up. I think there's room for 'em, too."

I skip back and forth from the house to the camper.

"Let's rest a spell," Mama says.

Papa opens a beer and I sit next to him at the kitchen table. I don't really want to rest. I want to get back to my playhouse. It's hard to keep still as I watch Mama heat up some bacon grease.

"You got ants in your pants, child?" Mama says laughing. "Don't kick your Papa with them swingin' legs."

I cross them tight under the chair.

"She ain't kicked me yet," Papa says. So I start swinging my legs some more.

"Best get this girl out and about. She's so full of the devil," Mama says. "Let's head on out, Larry."

"I wanna play," I say.

"In a while, Sandy. Mama and I have a surprise for you…in town."

Papa goes out back to pull the truck around and Mama tosses her apron over the kitchen chair. Mama dabs some spit on her finger and cleans a spot on my cheek.

"Come on, baby."

"The pan's cooking, Mama."

"It'll be fine. Get a move on."

In town the ice cream cone tastes so good that I lick it in little swipes, trying to make it last. Chocolate drips down my hand and I clean it with my tongue.

"You're a sight," Mama says to me. Papa fidgets on the park bench.

"Ain't it been long enough?" he asks.

"Hold your horses, Larry. Let's give it a bit more time. 'Sides Sandy's still eatin'."

Later, when we're crowded in the truck cab, Papa pulls out from the curb. A car horn blares. Papa slams his foot onto the floor and the truck stops fast. I almost hit my head on the dash board, but Mama grabs me back to her.

"Watch it, Larry. Everything's gonna be fine. You'll see."

When we start driving again, Mama says, "Something's wrong. I can see the smoke."

"What smoke, Mama?"

"The house is burnin' up. Flames lickin' like the fires of hell."

I stretch my neck up and look out. I don't see anything except passing trees.

We drive some more.

"I know it, Sandy. The house is gone."

Mama is awful smart I think. We aren't even close to home yet, but she sees the fire's flames.

When we turn down our road, Papa snorts. "The fire truck is there alright. Sure is."

"I knowed it. I just knowed it," Mama says.

I can't believe my eyes. The ground is black with ashes and smoke curls up and up. I look from Mama to the fire and back again. Mama does have a way of knowing things.

"Praise be, your playhouse is safe, Sandy. The old tool shed, too," Mama says.

Papa nods and musses my hair. I hold his hand real tight and watch the breeze swirl the ashes into the air.

Later, Mama finds clothes for me in one of the storage boxes. She pulls out an old camp stove and cooks for us in the yard.

"Right lucky to have all those things on hand," Mama says winking at Papa. "We're staying put this time. No moving, no sir."

So we live in my playhouse.

One day, a man drives up into the yard. He waves at Mama who's standing in the camper doorway.

"Who's that man?" I ask.

"It's the insurance man, baby."

Mama walks to meet him. He hands her a piece of paper.

"Money can't replace all the memories you've lost, Mrs. Townsend, but you should be able to put a roof over your heads."

Mama looks like she's gonna cry when she shakes the insurance man's hand. He pats her shoulder when he leaves.

We watch his dusty black car drive away. I can see him wave out his window. When his taillights disappear, Mama smiles wide and her false teeth look too big for her mouth.

A few days later, Mama has a used single wide trailer moved in and sets it right on top of the black ashes. It smells a bit moldy from sitting in a sales lot for a while and Mama wipes down the walls with pine cleaner.

"Almost like new," Papa says looking around the living room. Then he sits in his favorite fat cushioned chair that had been stored in my playhouse and smiles at Mama.

The very next morning, I hear Mama and Papa yelling. Papa shouts, "I won't have Al in my house." Mama tells him she has no choice. Papa slams the front door so hard that a picture falls from the trailer wall. Glass shatters across the floor. Mama sweeps it under the curled up tile in the corner of the front room.

"Mornin', child. Guess you already heerd. Your daddy's coming home."

Papa doesn't come home all day. I hope he won't come home with the sickness tonight. It's getting dark outside and I'm so tired, too tired to find a hiding place. I get a little more scared when I remember that Uncle Ely moved away and won't be stopping by.

I watch Mama fill the small bathtub with water. She turns up the hot water and steam rises covering the sink's mirror with clouds. I write my name in blocky letters smearing the surface.

"That'll take the chill out," Mama says as she twists the knob off.

Even in California, it can get cold in late December. I shudder as Mama pulls my dress over my head. Goose bumps raise on my skinny arms as Mama lowers me into the tub. At almost seven years old, I feel too grown up for Mama to be giving me a bath.

Mama is drying me off when a man walks right into the bathroom. His face looks gritty and is dark with whiskers, his eyes brown and flickering as he watches me. Mama wraps the towel around me real tight and clutches me close.

"Hello, son," she says.

My father is so big it's like he fills up the tiny room. He is lots bigger than Mama and taller than Papa. He smells like old socks and stinky pipe tobacco.

"I'm your daddy," he says. His voice is deep and rumbling. He leans to kiss me, but I twist away and bury my face in Mama's neck.

"You'll scare the child," Mama says. "Leave her be."

My father's laughter rustles through the room like a ragged wind. Mama's neck is warm and damp.

"She's grown up to be a pretty little thing what with those blond curls and blue eyes."

"Reckon so. Make yourself to home while I take Sandy to bed, son."

In the shadows of the bedroom, Mama tucks me under the covers and presses her lips to my cheek.

"Sing me a song, Mama."

"Not tonight, child."

"Aren't you comin' to bed now?"

"I'll be in after a bit," Mama says, pushing my hair away from my eyes. "I've gotta feed your daddy some supper first. He's had a long drive."

Mama disappears leaving me alone in the dark and I clutch the covers to my chin. I stare at the light shining under the closed bedroom door listening to my father's voice and wondering if Papa will come home with the sickness. I don't sleep until Mama crawls in beside me and touches my cheek with her roughened hand.

The next morning, sun filters through the worn organdy curtains and I watch dust figures dancing in the air. The trailer house is quiet. No cooking sounds. No voices in the kitchen. Papa is probably collecting garbage. Mama must be outside. I dress and go looking for her.

The yard is empty when I jump off the wooden steps onto the gravel. The latest trash mountain is growing bigger. Rain has flattened the top of the pile and streaked dirty water stains like a waterfall.

I spot Mama across the wide yard where she's tending her roses. I call out but she doesn't hear me, so I dance and sway amongst the gravel and sparse weeds. I twirl around so the skirt of my blue cotton sundress flutters out and my hair bounces against my shoulders and back.

When I turn in fast circles, my skirt swirls higher and higher. I feel dizzy and giggle. When I finally stand straight, I hear a shuffling sound like paper scraping dirty linoleum.

Behind me, I don't see any movement at the hollow uncovered windows of our rusty trailer house. The slats of the screen door hug its frame and frayed mesh hangs still.

Far away Mama still hunches over her rose bushes. The red blossoms are bright against the dusty yard. A junky washing machine and a bunch of broken, old cars are on the other side of the gravel drive.

Again I hear the shuffling sound. Maybe it's a cat chasing a rat in the shed.

Then a man steps from the shed's shadows. My father's looking at me. He ambles forward and the soles of his moccasins grate against the sandy surface of the cement floor.

Turn away. Keep away. Too late, he motions to me.

"Come here," he orders. My father's voice sounds deep and harsh like coarse sandpaper.

When the trembling starts, I tighten my back and stand forward on my feet. Again he whispers his command.

Mama's words 'stay away from him, but don't make him mad' rush a warning to my head.

"Sandy, you heard me. Come here!" The words spew between clenched teeth.

My father motions again. Slowly, I walk across the gritty path toward the old shed. He moves backward into the shadows. I go to the doorway and adjust my eyes to the dimness. Piles of used lumber, a strewn toolbox, and rusted car parts fill the dark room.

"Over here, Sandy."

Behind a stack of worn rubber tires, his dark eyes peer at me. I walk in a circle around the tires. My father is sitting forward on an old, green metal lawn chair, its white arms chipped to the brown decay beneath them.

"Come over here, Sandy." Between short gasps of breath, he manages to change his voice from bossy to a purring tone.

When I am within a few steps of him, he reaches out and yanks me toward him. His hand grips the upper part of my arm and he clamps my body between his legs.

"I have to pee," I say.

"There's a coffee can right there," he motions with his head. His grip doesn't loosen.

"No, I want to go to the house. Please."

"I know your game. You won't come back." He chuckles. "Use the can."

"No, I…"

In a quick strong movement, my father swoops my sundress over my head and tosses it to the floor. When he jerks my panties down my legs, the elastic catches on the buckle of my white, dusty sandals and there is a ripping sound.

My father's face is slack, skin hanging loose on his dark bristly cheeks. His feverish, brown eyes hold the only light in the shadows.

He rubs my body against his legs. When I try to twist away, he sweeps me into the air and turns my body around so that he's looking at my back. His breath is hot air on my naked skin and I hear the metallic sound of a zipper easing down. Fear and his hand keep me high in the air. My feet dangle with nowhere to go.

Then the pain starts as he probes my bottom with something hard and stiff. I cry out, but his large hand clenches over my mouth and nose. I can't breathe. I'm gonna die.

"Be quiet. You don't want to get me in trouble, do you, Sandy?"

I sway when I try to shake my head. He releases the grip over my mouth then he raises and lowers my body over him. Something hard pounds against me again.

Pain shoots through me, from my bottom to my knees. Tears stream down my face as he bobs me up and down, up and down.

Over the stack of tires I see Mama tending her red roses. I pray that she looks up and sees into the shed's grimy window, but like always

Mama gently rubs the dew from the petals then moves over to the next bush in the row.

A voice breaks through the pain and tears. I hear my father say, "Daddy just wants to love you. Daddy just wants to love you."

CHAPTER FOUR

For the first time today, I feel safe as I curl up against Mama on the sofa. I rub my fingers back and forth in the folds of her cotton duster. Its red checks are nearly pink from so many washings.

Even though Papa smells like sour mash whiskey, he is quiet as he rocks back and forth in Mama's chair. My father is sitting in Papa's big chair with the soft cushions and saying, "No sir, nothing worse'n a narc. In the Joint or out."

"What's a narc, son?" Mama asks.

"Someone who rats out his buddy. Tells secrets." He looks at me when he says this.

I grab at Mama's skirt and nudge my head close to her side. She circles me with her arm.

Papa stops rocking and stares at me. Eyes once glazed are clear. His lips frown as he clutches the arm of the rocker and he looks from me to my father.

"You know how we deal with narcs in the joint, Larry?"

My grandfather shakes his head. Eyes leveled at Al.

"Well, in San Quentin, I helped some fellows chop up a sonuva bitch and stick his body into the water pipes. Helluva plumbing problem." My father laughs.

Papa turns his head and stares at me again. His eyes glisten like they're pools of water. The muscles in his arm look like someone let the air out of them with a pin.

"At Salem, we put a fellow into the concrete wall we was building in that new addition. Won't find him in a coon's age."

"That's enough, Al. You'll scare the child to death," Mama pleads.

"My little girl's no narc. She can keep secrets."

Papa's chair rocks faster back and forth. Back and forth.

Two days later, I stir the gravy in the big black skillet while Mama pulls biscuits from the oven. Papa moves the rocker into the kitchen and watches us cooking supper. My father is out back tinkering with an old car.

The rocker's wooden slats squeak every time the chair pushes back. I stay clear of the sharp edges that roll on the floor. Once I smashed my foot underneath and my big toe bled all over the place.

"Can't abide this headache, Opal. Bring me somethin' for it."

Papa rubs the sides of his head and moans ever so low. He shuts his eyes against the glare of the sun coming through the side window.

"Painin' a lot, Larry?"

Mama hands him some pills. "Chew these up."

"Baby aspirin. It's like orange chalk. Won't do no good."

"Better'n nothing."

"They're good for what ails you," I say like Mama always says to me.

Papa tries to smile, but then grips his head. His gnarled fingers clutch around his sunburned ears.

"We gotta get ya to the doctor, Larry."

"Don't need no doctor."

"It's badder than I ever seen. You could die or something."

Die? Papa die? Like the goldfish we buried under the lilac bush? The fish got so slimy it almost disappeared in the bowl water. Do people get slimy? Do their eyes pop out, too?

"Papa, don't die. Don't die."

Papa pats my head, starts to say something, then lets out a loud groan.

"Sandy, get your daddy. Tell him Papa needs a hospital."

After my daddy starts the car up, Mama helps Papa down the porch stairs. He walks clumsy like he has the sickness again. Should I hide alone?

"Get in the back with Papa, Sandy," Mama says.

What if Papa turns slimy or his eyes pop out?

I stand like a wooden figure next to the car door.

"Git on in, Sandy. Papa needs you." Mama's voice sounds end-of-the-day tired.

Inside, I slide as close to the car door as I can, but Papa reaches over, pats my lap, then lowers his head onto it. Sweat drips down the side of his face and circles around his ear where tiny white hairs are growing.

"Let's go, son," Mama says as my daddy backs out to the turnaround.

She reaches over the seat and rests her hand on Papa's shoulder. "Sleep'll do you good. We'll be to the hospital soon."

When the car eases onto the country highway, I watch what Mama calls worry beads drip down Papa's neck. I could wipe them off with the corner of my dress, but I don't want to touch Papa, not if he's really dying.

I tuck my right hand into the tight place between the seats and hold onto the flap above the rear window. Papa moans.

Green pastures fly by outside. I see cows munching grass and a horse nudging along the fence.

"There'll be white horses by a white fence when I go," Mama says. "Mark my words."

Go where? I want to ask Mama what she means, but Papa screeches and tries to raise up. When he falls back into my lap, his head is as heavy as a potato sack of dented cans. I start to cry and wriggle away from Papa's head.

What if his eyes pop out? I scream. The car stops and I yank at the door handle and bolt from the back seat. I scream so loud there is silence.

For the next two days, I live with the silence, shutting out all the words of the people coming in and out of the house. There's a few men from Daddy's new construction job, Uncle Ely, and some cousins. My real mother, Kristen, visits with Mama. They hold each other and cry. When Daddy walks up to them, I see the muscles in Kristen's jaw tighten.

"How's my favorite sister? You're looking mighty good," he says.

Her hands claw the sides of the wooden chair and she stares at the floor. Daddy walks over to her and caresses her shiny hair. She jerks her face away like she'd been burned by a hot poker. Daddy laughs before lumbering outside.

When Mama washes me and my hair, she says, "Baby, you gotta look presentable at the funeral home."

I don't want to see Papa dead. Mama drags me to the car. Later, she drags me up the church aisle to the casket.

Mama lifts me in her arms and tells me to look at Papa, saying how rested he looks. I peek through half-opened eyes. Papa is sleeping inside a white silky cloud. He's not slimy and I'm glad his eyes are closed.

His cheeks are a bright pink against the rest of his face that is as white as his hair. His lips are pink, too, like the plastic Kewpie doll that sits on top of a shelf in the front room.

"Kiss Papa good-bye," Mama says.

Her hands are strong around my waist as my feet dangle high off the craggy wooden floor. My legs flail against Mama's belly. I twist back and hold her neck tight.

"No hugs now, baby. It's time to kiss Papa good-bye."

Her voice sounds funny like wood popping in the kitchen stove. She lifts me over the casket again.

As I get closer to Papa's face, I'm scared his eyes will pop open so I shut mine. My jaw is so tight I think my teeth might break off. When my face touches Papa's, I shiver. His skin is cold like a winter bed.

Mama whispers, "That's a good girl, Sandy."

Air rushes to my ears as my feet touch the floor. When I open my eyes, I see red and white flowers circling Papa's casket. Their sickening sweet scent clings to my nose and dress. Later that day, I hide the dress in the pile of trash by the back door.

When I sneak through the kitchen, I hear Mama crying.

"I spent two hundred dollars to bury the sonuva bitch. Why are you crying?" my father asks.

CHAPTER FIVE

Oregon, 1968

Wind whistles between the gaping wooden slats. Mama and I lay in our clothes under a pile of quilts and blankets on top of a tattered, bumpy mattress. The dirt floor is frozen hard. It is February in Bend, Oregon.

"I'm freezin', Mama," I say as I snuggle under Mama's arm. She pulls me close and we huddle with our heads beneath the covers. I wonder if we will smother under the heavy blankets. My body aches with the weight.

I miss Papa, the trailer, and California. So does Mama.

We left California the day Mama's Social Security check came in the mail. Daddy made her sign it, picked up money from the bank, and piled us into the car.

For miles Mama sat with Papa's old boot hugged in her arms. Tears rolled down her cheeks. Her lips quivered deep into her face. Since Papa died, she hasn't worn her false teeth.

"I'm tired of your whimpering, old lady," Daddy said as he pulled off the highway into a clearing. Leaning across me, he ripped the boot from Mama's lap.

"No, no, it's Larry's. I want it," Mama said tugging at Daddy's arm. Squashed between the two of them, I watched the boot wrenched from Mama and tossed out the car window.

"Was all I hadda Larry," Mama said. Arms open and empty in her lap.

"He was a good for nothing. Didn't even leave enough to bury hisself."

When the car eased onto the dark highway, I patted Mama's arm. Her chest rippled with silent crying.

Hours later, we parked in front of my Uncle Paul's house. It looked like a storybook picture with its pretty peaked roof. The house was painted a cloudy blue and the trim, a crisp white.

Inside, small rooms meandered throughout the house. The first few nights Aunt Molly, Uncle Paul, and Daddy let Mama and I sleep upstairs. We could hear their laughter and talking after we were ordered to our room.

It was just as well, because I was scared of Aunt Molly. Aunt Molly dressed in long evening gowns, some taffeta and lace, others sheer chiffon. She had a big closet of dresses. One day she gripped my arm and dragged me to that closet. When she yanked the double row of dresses apart, I saw a door with dent marks like it'd been hit with a hammer. She said, "NEVER EVER go in there, do you hear me, girl?"

I nodded fearful of her bulging eyes that gleamed with a devilish heat. I was never so curious that I disobeyed her. I thought hell was behind that door. Hell blazes brighter and hotter than the fires that had burned down all our houses.

At mealtimes, Aunt Molly set two extra places.

"Sandy, say hello to Satan." Aunt Molly pointed to an empty chair.

"Hello," I repeated softly.

"He didn't hear you. Say it again."

I did and she nodded. "Now say hello to Jesus." Aunt Molly pointed to the other chair across the table. Satisfied with my response, she told me to sit down next to Jesus and Mama.

"Why Jesus and Satan?" Mama asked.

"They've been fighting over me for years. Haven't you, boys?" Aunt Molly laughed and told us that Satan was winning. "Truth be told, right, Paul?"

"Right, honey," Paul answered patting her bony hand where yellowed nails grew so long that they curved under.

She smoothed back her white hair, yellowed from cigarette smoke, and began passing the dinner bowls around.

After Aunt Molly had taken a bite of the meat loaf and the vegetables, Mama nodded to me. Only then could I pick up my fork. Mama worried that Aunt Molly would poison us. She said we could die like Papa did.

After eating supper, Daddy told me to help Aunt Molly clean up the dishes. When the two of us were in the steamy back room, Aunt Molly whispered to me.

"You better take care, girl. Else I'll throw you down this hole."

After her threat, Aunt Molly leaned down and yanked up a trap door right in the middle of the kitchen floor. It was as black as her green-eyed cat that lurked beneath the dining room table.

"Look there. See anything?"

I shook my head.

"It's so deep it goes to hell." She threw down a beer bottle that made a whooshing sound when it finally landed in the well water.

I shivered and stepped back toward the sink. Aunt Molly laughed calling out to my daddy and Uncle Paul.

"Sandy, here, has seen hell. Haven't you, girl?"

"Leave her be, Hon. No sense scaring a little girl," Uncle Paul said. "Best go on up to bed, Sandy. That's enough for tonight."

I had fled to an upstairs room away from the white-haired witch. Mama told me, "Molly's tetched in the head. Crazier than a bedbug."

So when Aunt Molly, having discussed it with Jesus and Satan, said Mama and I had to sleep in the woodshed, I felt a little safer, away from the big closet and the pit to hell.

Now sleeping out back, I ask, "Mama, can't we go back to California?" My voice sounds small under the layers of covers.

"I wish we could, baby. I wish we could."

The next morning, Uncle Paul brings us out some food, a few slices of bread and a banana. "Sorry 'bout this, Ma."

I see a watery sadness in Uncle Paul's eyes when he brings food to us, when he pats Aunt Molly's arm, and when Aunt Molly sits in my daddy's lap. Before Uncle Paul leaves for work every day, he sits for a while in his truck watching the house. Then he drives slowly away to his job at the mill.

After Uncle Paul leaves, Aunt Molly, wearing a red evening dress and fur coat, walks down the front walk toward town. "Mama, look, there goes Aunt Molly. Can we go inside for a while?"

"Okay, baby, but just for a few minutes. Molly'll be back soon enough."

The house is warm and smells of roses. Aunt Molly has the florist deliver fresh flower arrangements every Wednesday. The bakery delivers at least one cake a week for her special dinners with Uncle Paul, my daddy, Jesus, and Satan.

"Go on and wash up, child, while I search the kitchen for some more food."

In the bathroom, I let the water run warm over my reddened hands. My fingers tingle when the water hits them.

I jump when the door opens and my daddy slides through, locking the brass knob behind him. Already I smell his morning cigarettes and coffee as he leans over to kiss me. Hands, callused from road work, scratch me as he lifts my dress over my head. His beard is hard like the bristles of a toothbrush when his face rubs down my body. If I wiggle away, he pushes harder against me.

A whimper escapes my lips. "Hush, baby girl. Daddy's just loving you some." Daddy's breath comes faster and faster until he groans loud and spills his stickiness into me.

"Wash up now. Best to keep our special secrets." Daddy leaves me naked and alone. I can hear him talking and laughing with Mama as I rinse his stink from me.

Minutes later, I find Mama and my daddy in the kitchen where she hands my daddy a mug of coffee. "Here you go, son." Steam rises from the top of the mug. Daddy sits at the table, leg propped over the edge. He's wearing his hard hat and heavy boots.

"Ma, I gotta get back to the road crew. So you best get back outside. Molly's due back soon," Daddy says. A smile curls up his lip as he nods his head toward the back door.

In the next few days, snow whirls outside our shack. Mama puts up a sheet on one side trying to keep the coldest wind from blowing through. The bread she has smuggled from the house is hard to chew, cold against my teeth.

"Someone's coming," Mama says. "Hide that bread." I stuff it under the layers of quilts, but its coldness seeps through my nightdress.

A flashlight shines on us first before Uncle Paul says, "See this here drop cord. It comes from the house. I got this cord rigged to the out-house. Heat lamp'll warm it up for you once you plug 'em together."

"Thank you, son. It's mighty cold out here. Mighty cold."

"I know, Ma. I'll try to get you an electric blanket on payday." Uncle Paul hands Mama a thermos and turns to leave.

"Wait, son. What's in the thermos?"

"Hot coffee. Molly made it."

After he leaves, Mama plugs in the cord. "Go on, baby. See how the heat works."

I cover my shoes with plastic bags and Mama walks outside the shed with me. She loosens the lid on the thermos and pours the coffee onto a pile of snow. Smoke rises where it lands and spreads dark, melting the mound.

I scurry down the trench-like ruts that Mama and I scraped out with a board. There is a light in the outhouse, warming the inside. Sitting between the two wooden holes, forgetting the horrid smell of human waste, I turn my face up toward the light pretending it is the California sun, that I'm combing Papa's hair, and that my stomach is full of bologna sandwiches.

CHAPTER SIX

"You gotta start earning your keep," Daddy says after we had parked in the off road clearing. "Grab them gas cans. Let's go."

The biting mist chills my nose that starts to drip, wet and sticky against my upper lip. When I lift my gloved hand to swipe at it, I clang the can into my chest. Daddy's silent glare warns me to keep quiet.

Daddy carries four gas cans, crouches down and peers through the scraggly hedges clinging like balled up yarn to the barbed wire fence. "See that big green tank? That's where we're headed. Keep close to me, you hear?"

I nod following behind him across the field toward the back of the low, flat farmhouse. I can hear Daddy's soft-soled boots squish through the mud. I try to step into his deep, size eleven crevices. When I miss, the mud sticks to my black rubber rain boots that feel heavier and heavier with each step.

The metal tank has chips of paint missing and towers over me. Daddy rigs up tubing from the spout end of the huge tank.

"Put this in your mouth and suck," he says.

A thick liquid like hardening bacon grease storms into my mouth, its stink rises through my nose. I gag and spew it out. The odor lines my throat like slimy chicken fat.

Daddy's rumbling laugh hits the sides of the tank like pellets as he puts the hose back into my mouth.

Daddy pulls off my glove and says, "Sip a little out and put it into your hand."

Spit and gasoline ripple in my palm. Nausea turns my stomach upside down. I want to throw up.

Daddy dabs his finger into the gasoline circled in my hand and rubs his thumb and finger together. He touches his tongue to his fingertip.

"Diesel," he says. He unhooks the syphon and we loop behind the barn toward the truck and car sitting side by side. Again he connects the hose and fills two of the gas cans from the gas tank of the car then moves to the truck.

Both times I taste the gas. The regular gas tastes stronger, but not as slick as the diesel. As we head away from the barn, a bright light shines out from the house.

"Damn it to hell," Daddy mutters under his breath.

I can see the black shadow of a man outlined on the porch. There's a shotgun at his side. Daddy hunches next to the bed of the truck watching the man. He motions for me to follow him around the side of the barn.

The one gas can that's full is heavy and sloshes when I walk. It bangs into my knee and I bite my lip so I won't cry. I stumble over a pile of 2 x 4s and drop both gas cans. One clangs like the hollow coffee can that Daddy uses for target practice.

"Get the hell off my land you stinking thieves! I'll blow you to kingdom come!" The farmer's angry voice echoes in the vacant countryside.

I hear a door slam and Daddy moves quickly in a circle pattern through the field and back to the car. I run fast behind him, hands empty and the taste of gas filling up my throat.

At the car, Daddy tosses his gas cans in the trunk and slams the trunk lid real hard. "You stay put," he orders me. "I'm gonna hurt that sonuva bitch." His threat rests deep in his throat.

I scrunch up in the back seat hiding under a heavy woolen blanket. I don't want the trees looking at me or that farmer to come up and blow my head off. As the sound of Daddy's footsteps disappear, I roll onto the back floorboard.

My head hurts so bad and I want to throw up, get the horrible taste out of my mouth and the tightening pain out of my stomach. I want to cry. I want to go home. Mama would know how to make the ache go away.

My stomach rumbles like the start of a truck engine. It turns over and over. A low moaning visits the back seat of the car. I shudder and realize the moan comes from deep inside me.

I am doubled over when Daddy slams the trunk then opens the car door. "Showed that sonuva bitch. He won't be bothering nobody else."

I hear him shifting his weight. The front seat creaks when he looks over the back for me. "Get outta that blanket and up front with me," Daddy says.

Moaning is my answer. Daddy laughs. "You'll learn soon enough, girl. You taste it, don't drink it. Makes you sicker than hell."

I whimper like a kitten missing its mama.

"You ain't gonna die so get on up here."

Hours later in the woodshed, Mama cuddles me to her. "You be too young to be syphoning gasoline."

A heaviness sits like a bucket of rocks in my stomach pushing against my belly walls. Then the pressure moves downward and I run toward the outhouse. I almost make it. I spend the night and the next afternoon racing back and forth from the shed.

That night Daddy comes out back and says to me. "Well, girlie-girl, guess you learned a thing or two about what not to swallow."

"Al, let her be. She's still a young 'un," Mama says.

"I know what she's old enough for, old woman. Tomorrow we're heading for South Carolina to visit some old prison buddies of mine. I'm counting on both of you to do as you're told. Good training for Sandy. Time she helped her daddy out."

The next morning Molly hangs on daddy's car door. "Don't go away, Al. I need you here." Tears streak the fuschia rouge on her drawn cheeks. Her pink taffeta dress looks garish in the August sunshine.

"Go on, now, girl. We'll be back soon enough."

Molly grabs Daddy's face and presses her lips against his mouth. Then she glares across the front seat at me.

"Satan knows you're taking this whore child with you. Bad luck will be traveling with you all the way to South Carolina."

"Sandy's my baby girl, Molly. She's my lucky piece." Al laughs louder than he should. Molly's face shades redder than her rouge. Mama snorts with disgust from the back seat.

"Why your big brother Paul brought that baggage home from the Mustang Ranch, I'll never know," Mama says.

"You're right, old lady. You'll never know."

Molly doesn't look like someone who lived on a ranch, not with her fancy dresses and all.

"How can you ride horses with long dresses on?" I ask.

"She rides real good," Daddy says.

Mama snorts. Daddy looks in the rearview mirror at Mama and a smile circles his teeth.

The car trip is filled with stops and starts, what daddy calls 'lessons for Sandy.'

"Never leave a trail. You hear me, Sandy. We don't stop at any gas stations for gassing or peeing. No one knows when or where we are."

We syphon gas from the farmlands of Oklahoma and Kentucky. We shoplift food from grocery stores.

And we play EAT & RUN. Sambo's is Daddy's favorite restaurant. A billboard for Sambo's sets him to chuckling.

Stopping one night, Daddy yanks up the emergency brake and stretches his long legs out of the driver's door. "Come on, Sandy. Time for food and games."

"I'm hungry, son. Lemme go in this time," Mama pleads. Her voice sounds shrill in the late night air.

Daddy leans over the car seat and says in that deep voice he musters when he won't hear no back talk. "You disgust me, old woman. No teeth. Fatter than a pig at gutting time. Besides you're too slow to play the game with us."

"Don't worry, Mama. I'll bring you something good. A surprise. Okay?" I can see her lips quivering as she nods to me. Light from the flashing Sambo's sign flickers on her sunken mouth.

I skip into Sambo's. I love the wall mural with Sambo circling the pancake pile. Little Black Sambo is so lucky to have his picture on the walls and the menus. Daddy says he's the luckiest nigger around.

Dad talks real friendly-like with the waitress. She smiles wide showing a gap between her two front teeth. Her stringy brown hair clings to her head and a pencil sits on top of her ear.

"What's good tonight?" Daddy asks. "Other than you, honey."

The waitress blushes. Daddy says women all like flowery talk. You can talk a woman into anything with the right words, he always says.

"Your little girl is a pretty thing. As pretty as her mother?" The woman puts the eraser end of the pencil in her mouth waiting for my daddy's answer.

He pulls me close to him and lowers his head. "She's the spitting image of her mama. Her mama died two years ago."

"I'm sorry," the waitress mutters tightening her lips to stop the smile from edging up.

The pancake stack has butter oozing between each cake. I pour the syrup over the top and watch it slither down in pools around the side. I eat real slow to make each sweet bite last.

The waitress keeps walking by and my daddy winks at her. She gives me extra orange juice saying how a growing girl needs her vitamins. Daddy smiles his thanks.

"Now you go get washed up, Sandy," Daddy says. His signal for me to take Mama's biscuits and gravy to the car. The aluminum foil shines under the neon lights in the parking lot.

Moments later, Daddy lopes to the car and starts the engine. He laughs softly as we pull out onto the highway.

"You did good, Sandy girl. Real good."

In the back seat, Mama gums her biscuits as we travel on to South Carolina. Daddy pulls me close to him and puts his fingers under my skirt.

CHAPTER SEVEN

"Son, you better tell that gal the truth. She keeps callin' and I don't know what to say," Mama says. I can hear the sadness in Mama's voice.

Dad props his foot on the kitchen table. His waffle-soled boots look huge dangling in the air. His hard hat tilts back on his head.

"Tell her whatever you want, old woman. She'll quit calling soon enough. Now get me some of that coffee."

Mama uses a pot holder to pick up the coffee pot. It's an old metal camping one. Mama swears it makes the best coffee. She pours it into a glued-together white mug. Daddy slugs it down. "Hot and black. Just like I like my women," he says. He chuckles, never tiring of his saying. I figure Daddy has a truckload of pet phrases he can drag out when he needs one.

"Back to the subject, son. That woman's gonna leave her husband 'cause of you. Tell her you won't be going back to Carolina." Mama shakes her head.

"She'll figure it out soon enough."

I remember Daddy kissing the woman, cuddling her baby boy, saying how lucky that woman's husband was to have her. He had told her he wished he had a woman like her. Someone to love him and take good care of his orphaned daughter. She had cried in his arms the night we left. He blew her a kiss and said, "Soon, my love, soon." Then we drove back to Oregon.

The poor lady sounds sad on the phone when she asks for Daddy. I say he's not home, like he tells me to. Daddy makes other people sad, too. My real mother's voice would quiver whenever Daddy was around. Uncle Paul looked like he wanted to cry when Aunt Molly sat on Daddy's lap.

When we returned home to Oregon, Daddy moved the three of us into a two-bedroom house in Dallas with a screened-in back porch. He said it reminded him of the Carolina house where his prison buddy lived.

The phone rings again. Mama tells the sad lady that Daddy's not home and yes, she gave him the message.

Daddy's working construction regular. He says that being in prison kept his working skills up. He ran heavy equipment in San Quentin, Alcatraz, and Salem, plus smaller jails and work camps in between. Remember, baby, how I walled up those men, he reminds me. Dead men can't tell secrets, he says.

At night when I lie in bed, listening to Mama's quiet snores, I wonder about the men in those prison walls. Were they alive when Daddy put them there? Could they live for long? Was the concrete wet and heavy? What if the walls fell down? Most of all, I wonder if Daddy would put me in a wall if I told anyone our secrets.

When Daddy left on his road jobs, Mama and I would live more like normal people. She would pack me a lunch in a brown sack and I would ride a school bus into town.

During those times, I didn't fear the nights. No husky whispers, no prodding hands, and no threats turned to hushed sounds of loving. Just Mama's fleshy body lying next to mine in bed.

It was on one of Daddy's road trips when he sweet-talked yet another woman. That time the road camp's whore ignored Al's protests and showed up one fall morning. She drove into the front yard, beeping the car horn. Her dirty brown station wagon was loaded with her life's remnants, and a daughter.

"This here's Jolene." Daddy introduces the girl to me and Mama. Jolene edges behind her mother's pant leg and watches us with slate green eyes. Curly ash blond hair falls to her protruding shoulder blades. Smudges of dirt streak her pale skin.

"I'm Jane," the older woman says through brilliant red lips. Mascara has smudged her sun-freckled face.

Mama mumbles something akin to nice-to-meetcha and I stare at the two strangers who have come to share our house, a house already too small for the three of us.

A week later Jane solves the room shortage by shoving a lumpy mattress and an electric blanket onto the back screened-in porch. "You two'll be sleeping out here. Jolene will take the front bedroom and Al and I will share the other."

That night Daddy scrapes on the wire screen and motions me to follow him to his truck. Mama keeps sleeping and shifts under the blanket, blocking the cold November air from her wrinkled face.

I ease out of the screen door, careful to keep the creaking sounds at bay. Daddy walks with long-legged strides toward the truck cab. Inside we slide down into the seat, vinyl and dust smells mingle with the odor that is Daddy-Camel cigarettes and unbathed skin slick from a slathering of Old Spice. Tonight there is another scent, Jane's Tabu cologne. I want to gag and cry out. Instead I let Daddy touch me with his hands and clutch mine against his manhood. When the white, stickiness funnels up, he wipes himself with an oily chamois.

We lay on the truck's seat as Daddy catches his breath and begins rubbing against me again. I stare through the windshield at the night stars willing it to be over.

"Not a word to Jane or Jolene," he says. "Else you'll be out on the street or worse."

I nod and escape from the truck. I lope back to the porch and Mama. I can see Daddy's shadow in the truck and the red glow of his cigarette.

The next night Mama and I sit on the porch watching Daddy, Jane, and Jolene eating supper. Fried chicken and hot biscuits. Jolene licks the butter off her fingers and Jane smiles through the window at us. My stomach rumbles. My fists curl up tight and I think of smashing Jolene in the face. Right then she turns and looks at me, a slight curve lifts her thin lips into a smile.

Mama curls back under the blanket and turns the control setting higher. Later, I will ride Jolene's bicycle into town and scrounge for food. Our stash, hidden in the old chicken roost out back, is double wrapped in aluminum foil. It has dwindled to bread crust and a bruised orange.

As I ride to town, cutting through the back roads and across a weeded field, I like the feel of the wind against my face and forget the tightening of my belly. I am an eight-year-old pirate searching the garbage cans for hidden treasure.

CHAPTER EIGHT

The cigarette dangles from Daddy's mouth and smoke drifts upward to the gray fabric ceiling of the car. I listen to Mama's scratchy, rhythmic snores from the back seat. The trees stand in a circle around the clearing and look down at us like rows of plastic soldiers.

"Let's get out and stretch," Daddy says. He swings his legs around and stands tall like the soldier trees.

I scramble across the vinyl seat and scrape my knee on a tear in the seat cover. "Ouch," I say and rub the spot that stings.

"You're fine, Sandy. Now lookee here." Daddy rubs aside loose dirt with his soft-soled moccasins and draws a map on the ground. With a ragged stick, he scrawls a picture of the targeted house and the land around it.

"Sandy, I'm gonna put you through the kitchen window...here." Daddy points as he talks. "You gotta climb off the sink and go back here and unlock that door."

I nod and picture the inside of the house with my nine-year-old mind. I imagine dark creatures, a mean dog, or even a hairy monster. A tingle of fear crawls up my body and rests like a big rock in my stomach.

"Then back you go to the front door. Stand watch until I give you the all-clear signal. Got that? Just like we practiced."

"Yes, Daddy," I say, but think that this isn't our backyard or our house.

"Now, if something goes bad, you get yourself out of there and get over to this road. There's a clump of trees. Hide there 'til I come for you. I'll flash the headlights then you can come out. If I don't get here by midnight then you start walking home."

Hide in the bushes, alone on this freezing night? My stomach turns over again and again as I think about hiding alone in the dark. I know he'll come back for me, if he can. If is such a scary word. I would have to walk to the main road and hitchhike. Daddy and I have talked it over before. Still, talking and doing is two different things, Mama says.

Daddy erases the drawings with the toe of his moccasin and slides back into the old white Ford that used to be a police car. He leans his head back and closes his eyes.

I lean against the car's front bumper and stare through the cottonwood trees. Across the wide, scruffy field, I know there is a narrow asphalt road that leads to the house we are going to rob.

"Git back in the car, Sandy," Mama whispers from the back seat. "You'll ketch your death."

When Mama wraps me in a wool blanket, she hugs me close. I wish I was cuddled with Mama in our bedroom. When Jane's husband, Sam, showed up last week, Jane and Jolene moved back in with him. Now that we have our very own room, I long to be in it and away from these woods and the scary hours ahead. Still, we wait for night to come.

When the sun hides behind the Cascade Mountains, Daddy lights a Camel and moves to the back end of the sedan.

I get out and join him. I'm cold and wish I were anyplace but here. It doesn't much matter what I wish, so I start to get ready. Daddy changes into fur-lined slippers that he bought in Coos Bay. He takes a short plastic comb, a handful of change, and a wallet from his pant's pockets before putting on his Army jacket. There are so many different pockets in it that I can't count that high yet.

As I slip into my jeans, the insides are cold. I shiver and put on my sneakers. Daddy stuffs my blonde hair into a black stocking cap.

"Inspection time," Daddy says. I stick out my arms and fingers to show him I don't have on any jewelry. "Good girl, can't have you getting caught up on anything."

My dark jacket is so fat. I feel like I'm wearing a balloon. Daddy zips it up tight. "Can't have nothing flapping or loose," he says.

Daddy hooks flashlights into our coat pockets. He hands me a pair of leather gloves that have to fit like a second skin, he says. He lifts his jacket up and slides a gun under the front of his pants.

Before closing the trunk, Daddy leans in and says, "Okay, Granny, you stay here and wait. Don't leave and don't make no noise. Hear?" Mama nods and slumps down in the seat. I can only see the top of her hair.

"Here," Daddy says and hands me a hard candy from the upper left pocket of his jacket. It's a striped peppermint and tastes good in my dry mouth.

Hand-in-hand we walk through the trees away from Mama and the clearing. Across the big field is the long, low house where Daddy says the rich people live.

When I look back over my shoulder, I see the row of trees, but can't see the car or Mama anymore. Daddy and I walk real slow across the muddy field of thick wild grasses.

"Gotta keep moving just right," Daddy says. "That way no headlights can spot you."

My heart pounds harder and harder as we get closer to the road. First, we settle into a ditch and hide so Daddy can watch the street, the house, and the neighbors. Big fields of farmland separate them.

"The house is still empty," Daddy says. He stands up and pulls me to my feet. We cross the gravel country road to the front yard. My stomach hurts deep down and I want to throw up. But I walk with Daddy up the path and into the bush-covered alcove. Daddy removes a long, bent screwdriver from his jacket pocket and flips up the window lock.

"Up you go," he says and lifts me through the dark opening. It's like a cave with a slippery floor. I am standing in a kitchen sink. I try to scrunch up my body real tight so no one can see me. There is a humming sound coming from the refrigerator and I search the darkness. My eyes are dry from looking so hard.

Sliding down from the sink top, I land with a thud on the linoleum floor. I feel my way along the cabinets toward where the back door is supposed to be. My foot hits something and it sails across the floor hitting the wall with a clanging sound. I freeze and try to breathe. Finally, I see a metal dog dish rammed under the cabinet edge.

I breathe in gasps waiting for the dog to attack me. I hear a scratching sound. My chest tightens as hard as the candy I'm sucking. It's Daddy at the back door. I race to the lock and let him inside. Right then I am glad that he is as tall as the trees.

"What was that racket?"

"A dog dish," I whisper.

"Get to that front door," he says. Then he does his run-through of the house.

The front room was so big and dark I thought it would swallow me up. I peek through the small opening in the front door watching for any slowing headlights and listening for voices. Nothing. Then all of a sudden two round lights come down the road toward the house. They pass quickly and I finally breathe when I see their red taillights.

"All clear," Daddy says. I shudder with relief to hear him. Even though it is a strange house, I feel safe with Daddy here.

"There's jewelry in the front bedroom. Check for a money stash like I taught you. Quick now, Sandy. Get a move on."

A tiny dog that looks like a dust mop follows at Daddy's heels. He reaches down and scratches the top of the dog's floppy ears. "Found her hiding under the bed." Daddy is proud of his way with animals. Daddy's not afraid of anything or anyone.

"Get busy. It's work time," Daddy says and I run to the front bedroom. I strip the pillowcase off the bed and remake the top. Daddy says I should not leave a trace. A three drawer jewelry box rests in the center of the dresser. After opening it wide, I scoop the rings, earrings, and necklaces into my cloth bag then put the box back together.

After sliding out every drawer and searching under their rails, I smile when I find an envelope taped to the underside of a center drawer. I throw it in fast and know I'll get to see what I found later. There's more money under the woman's silky panties. Daddy will be happy with me.

"About through?" Daddy calls in a husky whisper.

"Almost." I flip through the bedside books quickly. No luck.

In the dark hallway, Daddy grabs the pillowcase from my hand and says, "Get some towels from that closet and bring them to me in the dining room."

I pile them high in my arms and set them on the table top. It's shiny and pretty like it's been cleaned lots of times.

Daddy props open two suitcases and wraps silver spoons, knives, forks and a tea service in the towels. Between them, he packs fancy glasses.

"Business time is over. Let's get these outta here."

Daddy carries the suitcases and my filled pillowcase toward the back door. "Grab that clock off the mantel, Sandy."

The mantel is high and I have to stand on tiptoe to reach the clock. Daddy will have another clock to add to his collection. Mama and I don't like the sound of all the dings every hour of every day, but Daddy smiles when they chime and every once in a while he strokes the sides of one and looks like he's far away.

The scraggly dog watches us leave.

Daddy carries everything across to the drainage ditch by the mailboxes and lines them in a row. Damp grass shifts to hide them from the street.

"Now, its fun time," Daddy says with a chuckle and grabs my hand. I skip beside him back to the house.

Chapter Nine

On the television screen, a woman screams in pain while a doctor tells her to push and push again. "Why isn't the doctor helping her?" I ask.

"He is, child. The woman's having a baby." Mama pats my hand and keeps watching the program.

I can see the sweat shine on the lady's face that twists with agony before each cry. "I can't do it. I can't," the television lady yells. I cringe beside Mama.

I never want a baby, I think to myself, not if it hurts so much. I wonder how you know when you're gonna have a baby. Later I ask Mama.

"First off, you hafta to be with a man. He gives you his seed then you gain a lot of weight while the baby grows inside. I used to pee all the time when I was carryin' a baby. I carried my share of young 'uns. Yessir."

"How do the babies get out?"

"From your private place. That's where the seed is planted, too."

There? There, where Daddy puts his hands and where Tall Timber sprays me with white stickiness? I better not tell Mama about that. Daddy says it is our special secret. He even has a nickname for my private place, Baldy.

Over the next week, I weigh myself every day. I also keep count of how many times I pee. When the scale says I weigh two pounds more, I start crying. I can't seem to stop. I huddle in the bed clothes and try to hide from Mama.

"What is it, child? What's wrong?"

I don't want Mama to ask me. I can't tell her. I know what Daddy does to people who tell secrets. I cry even more wishing I could disappear into Mama's arms and never come out again.

"There's nothing you can't tell your Mama. How can I make it better, if you don't tell me?"

The longer Mama holds me, the safer I feel. Her arms encircle me like a strong fence, keeping out everything bad.

"Tell Mama now. Everything'll be okay. I promise." Mama's words are softer than a feather pillow.

"I'm gonna have a baby," I say.

Mama gasps and a trickle of laughter escapes. "What in the world makes you say that, child? You cain't be having no baby. Ya just a baby yourself. My nine-year-old baby."

She pulls away from me and wipes the tears still slithering down my face. "Stop the crying and tell Mama where you came up with such a notion?"

"I'm getting fatter, Mama. And I pee all the time."

"Sweet baby, you be too young. Besides you don't have no man's seed in you."

Then I tell her about my daddy and his loving me so much. Her eyes cloud over with fury.

"Anybody see you and your daddy? Was the curtains drawed?" Mama's voice sounds shrill like a train whistle. She doesn't wait for me to answer. She paces the room, muttering about my daddy doing it again.

Then Mama cries out and clutches her chest. At first, I'm not too worried. She's done the same thing in the welfare office when they've said they'll cut off our food stamps or our welfare check.

But when she collapses and vomits all over the linoleum floor, I get real scared. Her face starts to turn a bluish color and I remember her medicine. Her tobacco pouch hangs between her breasts, I reach under her dress and yank it out, take a small pill, and stick it under her tongue.

That's when I stand and rush for the phone. My bare feet are wet from the pee that comes out from under Mama's skirt.

Mama's in the hospital for seven days. Daddy moves me into his bed and talks of secrets and people dying.

"Mama might die because of your lies, you know. You scared her to death."

When Daddy leaves during the night, I am afraid to sleep. Tree branches scratch the windows like Aunt Molly's long yellow fingernails. Sometimes I see faces staring at me, shadows in the darkness.

Daddy peeks in people's windows all the time. He calls them his rounds, like a doctor makes. He watches them loving each other and when he watches he plays something called pocket pool.

I hear rustling in the bushes outside. Right now, I even wish Jane and Jolene were here. I'm so alone. What if it's Daddy staring in at me. Watching.

Snuggling deeper into Mama's patched quilt, I can smell her, the leather of her tobacco pouch and the scent of her rose scented toilet water. I pretend Mama is beside me keeping me safe from the strangers outside and my daddy. What if she dies because I told her my daddy's secrets? I'll never tell again, I say over and over like a nursery rhyme. I'll never tell again.

It's on a Monday when Mama comes home. She looks tired and her gums sink even deeper into her mouth. I run to hug her, but not too tight, she looks like she could break.

"You be safe now," she says. "Mama's home."

After I'm in bed, I hear Mama and Daddy arguing in the kitchen.

"You ain't ever gonna do it again. You heer me, Al. She's just a baby. She's your baby. It be a sin against God to be messin' with your very own child, your flesh and blood."

"You shut up, old woman. I'll leave here and take Sandy with me. You'll never lay eyes on her again."

There's a muffled sound like Mama crying.

"Who you gonna tell? Huh? Who? Who'd believe a crazy old woman?"

I hear pounding like Daddy is hitting the table with his fist. My own fists grab the covers up over my head.

"You just leave her be. Leave her be."

The screen door slams hard and the pick-up truck spits gravel when it drives away. I slip out of the bedroom and find Mama with her head on her arms crying at the table. I rub her back soft-like.

"It's not gonna happen no more, Sandy. I'm gonna call your other mama and get custody."

"What's custody?" I ask.

"That's when you be all mine. Legal like."

"I'm already yours, Mama. Haven't seen my real mama since the funeral."

"Well, that's so. Your daddy ain't gonna hurt my grandbaby no more."

Mama pats her lap and I crawl up. I cuddle against her and she strokes my hair while she croons her favorite song.

> *The owl and the pussy-cat went to sea*
> *In a beautiful pea-green boat.*
> *They took some honey, and plenty of money*
> *Wrapped up in a five pound note.*
> *The owl looked up to the stars above,*
> *And sang to a small guitar,*
> *O lovely Pussy, O Pussy, my love,*
> *What a beautiful Pussy you are,*
> *You are,*
> *You are,*
> *What a beautiful Pussy you are.*

(Edward Lear, "The Owl and the Pussycat")

CHAPTER TEN

The car roars under me. When I move the steering wheel, I can make the car turn all directions, even in circles if I want. My hair blows in Daddy's face because I'm sitting in his lap and he's working the pedals.

"You're doing real good, Sandy. Not much longer and you'll be reaching the pedals all by yourself."

Dust swirls behind the car as I steer down the dirt road. I figure this is what flying feels like. I wish Daddy would let me go faster and faster.

When I drive into the yard, Mama's dog Tinker barks and yips. Mama grabs the terrier up and holds her tight.

"Don't that dog beat all?" Daddy says. "Yappy three-legged little varmint."

"You be comin' in for supper?" Mama calls across at us.

"In a little while. Sandy and I got some work to do." Daddy pops the hood. "We're gonna change out the water pump. See here. This is the radiator. We have to drain this before we take it out to get to the water pump."

Daddy points to the boxy-looking radiator. A green gook comes out. Daddy says the gook is water and antifreeze. In cold weather, the antifreeze keeps things from freezing into ice. The grease sticks to my hands. I wonder if you could make hand prints with it like you can with finger paint. Everything looks so close together and Daddy's hands are so big. My hands fit easier so Daddy lets me take the fan out. Daddy shows me what he says is the pump assembly. There are so many names to remember.

"Sometimes hose clamps and bolts can be real tight and hard to get off. You'll get stronger and stronger. You'll be able to do these jobs as good as your Daddy."

When Daddy teaches me about the car and I get to work with him, I forget everything else. I feel so smart when he says I'm a quick study.

"Hand me a crescent wrench. It has a handle like a table knife and the top looks like a doughnut that you've bit in two."

I pick through Daddy's big metal tool box. There are a lot of tools with handles like that. I take out one and hand it to Daddy.

"You're half right. It is a wrench, but it's a pipe wrench. Try again."

On the third try, I find the right one. I say, "It looks more like a picture of the moon in my old book where the cow jumps over it."

Daddy asks for a screwdriver and I find it right away. It's just like the one he has for the burglaries.

"You knowing how to drive and how to fix cars'll be a big help to me on the job. We're gonna make a mechanic outta you yet."

A few weeks later, Dad, Mama, and I head for the Columbia Gorge. It's Friday afternoon and Daddy's off work for the weekend. He says his real job is hitting houses. He plans all week and then we take off.

"Gotta drive a long way from home when you rob people's houses. Don't do no real business in your own hometown."

Daddy never sleeps except for his cat naps. He can drive for hours and hours, never getting tired. He smokes his cigarettes and weaves through all the back roads finding his way to the houses he wants to case.

He lets me sleep a lot of the way, but he always has me in the seat next to him and has to be touching me all the time. Sleeping keeps me from having to get in his lap, so sometimes I pretend and keep my eyes shut real tight. Mama stays quiet in the back seat.

She's his cover, Daddy says. Who would suspect a middlin' old man and his toothless mother of being robbers? So far he's been right. No 'smokies' have stopped us yet.

On Saturday we cruise looking for the right houses. Daddy says you can't drive too slow because you look suspicious. He likes one story ramblers because they're easier in and out. Less likely to be trapped, he says. He watches for piles of papers, outdoor lights on too early, and stuffed mailboxes. The further away from town, the better.

When we drive back by, he chooses house A and house B. After we find a good hiding place for the car, we wait until nightfall. We've parked up to three miles away some nights. It's sure a hard walk back to the car. Sometimes we're carrying suitcases, bags, pillowcases, and our Army jacket pockets are always full.

Tonight these houses are spread far apart. Daddy is especially happy about things.

"Love this Gorge area. Money and wide-open spaces."

Daddy sticks me through the doggy door of the first house. It's deadly quiet. I stand still listening real hard. Like usual my stomach is doing flip-flops. I want to have mouse ears like Daddy's, but I don't want my ears to ever be as big as Daddy's.

I unbolt the back door and Daddy slithers through. I don't know how such a big man can be so quiet. It's like the soles of his moccasins raise him into the air.

He motions for me to go to the front window while he does a run-through. I can see pretty good because the people left their porch light on.

"All clear," he whispers. "It's business time."

I breathe again. My stomach stops grumbling and I feel the rush of excitement. I'm a hunter searching for gold.

Daddy is real excited when I find a safe in the bedroom closet. He sends me off to gather up the Hummel figures while he opens the safe. We pack the jewelry in between towels from the master bathroom.

Daddy whispers that the jewelry is the genuine article and he should get top dollar for it.

I've wrapped the figurines in napkins from the dining room and packed them in a suitcase I found in the hall closet. I grab a small clock from a glass shelf in the living room. It has a dome over it and plays music when it hits the hour.

Daddy searches the pantry for coffee cans. He likes to store stuff in them at home. Sometimes he fills them with money, sometimes hard candy.

Under the sink I find plastic and paper shopping bags. I fill one with a jar of peanut butter, bread, a knife, and a container of what looks like fried chicken. The other sacks I leave by the door for when we come back inside.

We carry our bags across the road, over a fence, and into a pasture. Dad shoves them under a bush and we head back inside. Mama says she needs a new sweater and Jane wants a nice leather purse. Whenever Sam is out of town on a construction job, Daddy stays with her so I figure I'll find her a pretty one.

When it's fun time, I scout around for the items on our list. Daddy likes to find hunting knives, cameras, and sometimes he takes silly things like one slipper or a woman's nightgown. He says it drives the people nuts.

"It's almost ten, Sandy. Let's get moving."

If Daddy's not sure the people are out of town, we always start at eight and leave by ten.

The pasture looks wider than it did when we walked over. My shopping bags drag on the ground. The grass is wet so one gets a hole in it. Daddy scoops up the clothes that fall out and tie them in a knot around my neck. He grabs the other sack and hoists it up over his shoulder. Daddy is so strong, he can carry four suitcases without even breathing heavy.

Mama peers through the back window while Daddy and I load the trunk. He stuffs his jacket and the loose clothes under the suitcases. I take the food into the car with me.

"Get me my sweater?" Mama asks. I nod and smile. I also found a nice warm robe for her, but it'll be a surprise.

I spread the peanut butter on the bread and hand it back to Mama, knowing she can eat it without her teeth in. Daddy pees next to the car like always, lights his Camel and gets in.

We drive slowly out behind the bushes onto the bumpy dirt road. Daddy won't put his headlights on until he knows nobody is looking for us.

Hours later, when we get home, Dad stacks slabs of deer meat, white freezer paper, and the jewels on the Formica table. He tells me what each stone is and we examine it in the glare of the overhead lights. He's teaching me what's good and what's junk, he says.

"You'll be my eyes someday, baby. You just wait and see."

I help Daddy wrap the meat for the freezer. He takes two steaks, puts a necklace and diamond earrings between them then tears off the white paper. The packages almost look like Christmas presents except for the black pen that says T-bone, ground beef, and ribs.

We pile them into the outside freezer like we're packing a long white box for mailing. Daddy keeps a ring and a gold watch to show the man who'll buy it all from us. He calls the man a fence. Funny name for an antique dealer.

The next night when Daddy comes home from his construction job, he sets his hard hat on the counter and runs his fingers through his oily hair. His hands are black from the paver. Deep rings of sweat make circles under the arms of his shirt. His odor almost wipes out the good kitchen smells.

Mama has cooked biscuits and gravy for dinner. I get out the paper plates. Mama hates to bother with real dishes. She says she played

Cinderella long enough when she lived with her relatives and her first husband.

Just as we sit down, the phone rings. Daddy answers it and says "I'll be a sonuva bitch."

He hangs up, grabs his hard hat, and tells Mama that the FBI is coming.

"Do what Mama tells you, you hear?" He rushes out the back door.

Mama tells me to sit down and finish my supper. While I'm eating, she says, "The police will be looking for Daddy so's we tell 'em he hasn't been home from work yet, you hear?" I nod and tear the center out of a slice of white bread. After I roll it into a tight ball, I take a big bite out of it.

"Baby, if they ask you anything, you cry. Don't say nothing, just cry."

Not long after, there's a loud pounding on the front door. Tinker yaps and almost topples over with just her three legs to balance her. Mama moves quickly across the room, lifts up Tinker to her bosom, and opens the door wide just when a man shouts, "This is the FBI!"

Mama cringes back against the wall. Her eyes are wide like she's real surprised. The men rush in. They're wearing black suits and ties just like on TV.

"Where is he?" one asks Mama.

"Who? Who ya'll lookin' for?"

"Al Martin. That's who. Now where's the jewelry?"

"Don't know nothin' 'bout no jewelry. Al's at work."

"Right!" another man snorts.

I cling to Mama's dress. The tears fall easily. I don't have to fake that. These men are rustling through all the closets, turning over the couch cushions, and searching the cabinets. Piles of Mama's newspapers and old magazines are knocked over.

"Some housekeeper," one man says to another.

"What do you expect from white trash? A Good Housekeeping Award?"

A man laughs. Another calls out.

"Lookee here, a freezer. Let's check it out."

They pile the freezer meat back onto the kitchen table where Daddy and I had wrapped it. I hide my face in Mama's skirts so they can't see how scared I am. This is even scarier than going into those strangers' houses all alone.

Two men rip the paper off the meat and toss it on the tile floor. They slam a few pieces against the edge of the sink.

"Frozen solid. Nothing here."

Three of the men pass by me and Mama. A fourth stops and says, "I know it's Al that did the heist in Oregon and the fur truck, too. Tell him we'll be back."

Mama locks the door behind them and leans her back against it. She sets Tinker back on the floor and smiles at me. "Ya did real good, Sandy. Your daddy'll be proud."

"Let's get this meat back into the freezer 'fore it thaws."

Mama laughs and starts re-wrapping the meat. I clutch the cabinet on the kitchen wall afraid I'll fall down since my legs are shaking so bad.

CHAPTER ELEVEN

"I'm bored. Can't we go on home?" I ask as we sit huddled in the pick-up truck. The seat is getting harder by the minute and I'm sweating so much that my bare legs are sticking to the vinyl seat covers. Even though the sun's gone down the heat has settled in the old truck cab.

"Listen up. That's the guy's red sports car over yonder and I'm waiting till he comes out."

We've been parked on the street for better than an hour. Before that we drove up and down every road in the rinky-dink town. When Daddy spotted the car, he checked the license number against a number in his notepad.

"What are we following this guy for anyway?" My throat is as dry as the dust covering our truck.

"Some things are better you don't know," Daddy says.

"At least can I go get a soda or something?"

"You're staying put, girl. Unless you want to sit closer to your Daddy."

He's watching the front door of the bar, but I catch the meaning in his words. I hush up and scrunch tight against the passenger door. He chuckles.

We've been following this guy around for nearly a week off and on. All I know is that he works in one of the tall office buildings, wears fancy business suits, likes steakhouses, and lives in a big house outside of town. Daddy writes down everything in his notebook, times, dates, everything.

The guy looks to be old, maybe thirty. He's sorta handsome like Mr. Novak on TV. His wife is a blonde. Daddy says she's a knock-out and he'd like to spend a few hours with her because it'd keep that pouty look off her face for good.

When he talks about the woman, he gets that stormy look in his eyes like he does when he orders me to the back shed or on our nighttime drives. I wonder if he peeks in the wife's window at night.

Finally, the man comes out of the bar. Another man is walking with him to the car. They talk a few minutes then our guy drives away. When the other man heads down the street, Daddy eases the truck from the parking space and follows the red sports car through town to the man's house.

Daddy draws a picture of the front of the house. "Stay put," he says then he gets out and walks down the block. I figure he'll be casing the house out. Usually, we don't hit two-story houses especially when they're so close together.

The front door opens in the house across the street from the truck. I slide down out of sight hoping they aren't coming to check me out. My throat gets drier and my chest tightens. I hear footsteps crossing the road and someone calls out, "Good Night." A car door opens, slams shut and an engine starts. Relief sweeps over me like it does when Daddy calls out, "all clear!"

When the truck door opens, I bang my head on the door handle. Daddy smiles what he calls his shit-eating grin. He fills in a back picture of the guy's house, putting some thicker lines around the back sliding door.

"Is that where we're going in?" I ask.

"You ask too many questions."

On Friday, a few days later, Daddy tells me to have the burglary kit ready for that afternoon. I figure we're going to hit that guy's two-story house.

After I pull the black bag out from the closet, I start gathering the supplies. The Ivory soap could be used to stop any oil leaks without hurting the car. The Wrigley's Spearmint Gum can plug gas leaks. Next to the deck of cards I set a few wooden clothes pins. If necessary, a clipped card over the gas line will blow air back over the gasoline to keep it from overheating. The foot-long screwdriver can help start the car by bypassing the battery.

After putting in the black leather gloves, two flashlights, extra batteries, and a black stocking hat to cover my blonde hair, I close up the bag. I set it on top of the two Army jackets. The kit's ready.

The two five-gallon gas cans are filled and ready in the shed. We'll load them in the car before we head out for the weekend.

When Daddy comes in from work, he looks worn out. He's grimy from the paving job and complaining about some inspector. "That peckerwood better stop messing with me. He don't know what can happen. Does he, old woman?"

"No, Al. Guess he don't." Mama hands him a plate of sandwiches and a cold glass of iced tea.

Daddy chews half the sandwich and gulps the tea before talking again.

"Inspectors have been known to downright disappear, haven't they, Ma?" Daddy drains the rest of his tea and hands the glass to Mama for a refill. "Well, haven't they?"

"So they have, son. So they have."

I imagine Daddy tossing a man down on the hot asphalt and rolling him over with the paver. I shudder and wish Daddy wouldn't talk so much. I figure it's probably just talk. I hope it's just talk anyway.

When we drive West out of town, I ask, "Where are we headed?"

"California. Haven't been to my old stomping grounds for a while."

"That guy we've been following lives the other way, doesn't he?"

"Don't pay him no never mind anymore, girl. He's done with. Eaten at his last steakhouse. Now get over here next to your daddy."

"Ah, Daddy, I want to look out the window awhile." I cross my fingers hoping.

CHAPTER TWELVE

A cloud of dust follows Jane's station wagon up the road to our house. I cringe at the sight of her. Bright red lipstick slashes across her harsh, angular face. She's alone. Where's her husband? Sam's showing up a while back saved Mama and me from more freezing nights and our starvation diet. Did she leave him again? Is she coming back to live with us?

"Where's Big Al?"

"Out back," I say, barring the doorway.

She turns and heads around the house. Mama's still dozing in the rocker so I can sneak to the back bedroom window to hear what's happening. Mama would skin me alive if she knew I was eavesdropping. She can't abide snoops.

The window's open, but the yellowed window shade covers me from view. I peek out.

Daddy nods at Jane and keeps tinkering with the van's engine. Whether it's the afternoon breeze or I've developed Daddy's mouse ears, I hear most of what they're saying.

"Well, Al, he's headed out to the California job site tomorrow-right outside Marysville. Hauling the old camper behind him."

Oh, no, what if she and Jolene are coming back here? I'm so busy worrying, I lose track of their talking.

"The insurance policy all set?"

"All in order. We need to start the ball rolling. The sooner, the better," Jane says as she encircles Daddy's waist with her arms. She snuggles against his back.

He keeps tinkering and mutters something. Jane pulls away and says, "Two cold ones coming up."

I scurry back to the front room, plop on the couch, and grab a magazine. Jane lets herself in, walks past me, glares at Mama asleep in the chair, and grabs two beers from the refrigerator.

She slams the front screen a good one waking Mama up. Mama's startled and searches the room, spots me then sees Jane's brown wagon out front.

"That one here again? What connivin's going on? Up to no good that one."

"She and Daddy are cooking up something. Heard 'em talking about insurance."

"Whose insurance?"

"Don't know, Mama."

"Not mine, that's sure. I ain't worth a plug nickel dead or alive." She laughs and starts rocking. Tinker cuddles deeper in her lap, almost disappearing in the folds of Mama's plaid cotton dress.

Daddy spends a couple of nights at Jane's place. I watch TV while Mama makes us hot cornbread in her iron skillet. It's almost like a vacation with Daddy gone.

"Don't reckon your daddy's gonna move there-with Jane I mean," Mama says as she lathers lard between a wedge of cornbread.

"Who knows what Daddy's gonna do?" I say wishing he would go away forever and praying he won't drag us with him.

Friday afternoon, Daddy shows up to trade his car for the van. The engine roars to life and he lets it idle while he tosses some clothes into a bag and grabs the burglary kit from behind the hot water tank.

"Be gone a spell. Me and Jane got some business up Marysville way."

"How long's a spell, son?"

"Just long enough to build a little nest egg," Daddy says. His chuckle rumbles almost as loud as the van's engine. "Jane's bringing Jolene to stay while we're gone."

"What a pain!"

"She's a little darling, a little darling. Reminds me of you at that age." His sneer hangs from his thick lips.

Several nights later, Jane and Daddy slam into the house. Jolene and Mama are asleep in the back bedroom. I'm curled up on the couch.

Jane's rubbing up against Daddy and he's unlatching his belt buckle. Then Jane sees me.

"You spying on us?" Jane says. "Get the hell outta here."

"Unless you wanna have some fun with us," Daddy says putting his hand down the front of his pants.

I jump up and race out of there. Jane laughs and calls out, "Better run, girl. Your Daddy's way too big for you to handle."

I cover my ears blocking out the moans and groans as best I can. When they start talking, I creep nearer the front room and wedge myself behind the bathroom door.

"God, Al, did you see his face when he turned around? His eyes were as big as saucers. He was scared shitless. You pushing his car. His shoving into reverse. You revving up the van. No match for you, Al." Jane's laughter echoes in the darkness.

"He probably shit his drawers."

"Gotta hand it to you, Al. You're a genius at this kinda thing. Waiting to pull up behind him after the engineer is out of sight then hightailing it before the caboose comes by."

"I do know a thing or two about planning and killing."

"We did it, Big Al. We did it! Couldn't be much left of him or the car. He hit the train dead on and it dragged him a mile at least."

Hidden in the shadows, a chill raises goose bumps on my arms. Somebody's dead. It's not just Daddy trying to scare me into keeping secrets. Who is it? The man we were following in the red car? Another road inspector?

"Helluva mess for someone to clean up." Daddy's chuckle is ice cold.

"We're the ones cleaning up. Insurance money'll be here before we know it."

"You better get home so you can get that phone call."

"One more beer and I'm outta here. I'll pick up Jolene tomorrow after I hear from the cops."

"Best be practicing your widow's tears."

"Crocodile tears. Sam's not worth real tears."

Their laughter drowns out my footsteps in the hallway as I crawl into bed with Mama and Jolene. I hear the refrigerator door, popping sounds when the beers open, and finally the front door closing

Hunched up on the bed's far side, I wait. When Daddy passes my door and goes into the other bedroom, I breathe a deep sigh.

Jolene is curled against Mama and even though I don't like her, I feel sad for her. She loves her daddy so much, she was so happy when he came back, and now he's dead. I see poor Sam trapped between Daddy's van and the railroad crossing gate. When he was smashed into the roaring train, there must have been awful screeching, scraping, and screams. Death sounds. I couldn't find any laughter in that.

The next afternoon, Daddy answers the phone.

"I'll be goddamned. I'll be goddamned," he says. There's background sputters from the other end of the phone.

"Who'd have figured that sonuvabitch'd still be kicking?"

Shrill sounds echo from the receiver.

"Hush up, Jane. No sense getting in an uproar. He couldn't see us. Our brights were on."

"Yeah, guess you'd best show up at the hospital."

Daddy shrugs when he hangs up.

"Jolene," Daddy calls out the screen door. "I gotta take you on home to your mama. Get in here and get your stuff together."

As they're leaving, Jolene clutches her teddy bear tight to her chest. Daddy grabs one of her hands engulfing it in his calloused grip. Her steps slow and shorten, but Daddy drags her alongside. She looks so tiny next to his six foot five bulk.

"Come on, baby girl, Uncle Al's gonna let you ride in his big van."

He lifts Jolene onto the front seat, strokes her blonde hair, and leers at me.

CHAPTER THIRTEEN

"I want you two out of the house tonight. Go to a hotel, go anywhere, just get out of here." Daddy says to Mama and me. "I'm having a party and I don't need any sour faces around."

"Son, we'll stay in the back bedroom outta your way. We don't mind."

"Listen, old woman. Take Sandy and get going." Daddy's jaw is set tight. I know Mama won't get anywhere with him. I head to my room to get a few clothes.

When we start out the door, Daddy throws me the keys to the truck. Now that I'm twelve, I've grown tall enough to pass for fifteen and can handle driving better than most. Once I drop off Mama at Uncle Ely's, I plan to pick up my girlfriend Darla and we can cruise 97.

Darla's mother would spit nails if she knew. Her mother works at an all night diner and has lots of cop friends. Daddy gets a kick out of that, my best friend having a cop-lover for a mother and her daughter running with a thief. I figure what Darla and her mother don't know won't hurt them…or me.

"I love to hear the engine roaring under me," I say to Darla.

"I love driving down 97 looking at all the guys. Look at that one, that gorgeous guy in the hot Impala."

All I can see is the back of Darla's head. Her honey-brown hair is long and straight just like it's supposed to be. Mine curls no matter what I do to it.

"That's all you ever talk about, Darla. Boys. Boys. Boys."

I like teasing her. She's the only girlfriend I've had for very long because we've moved so much. She's absolutely the only person I could ever joke with.

"What else is there except boys, boys, boys? You're such an ice princess. You'll probably be a virgin when you die."

My stomach tightens up and I want to scream at her that I haven't been a virgin for as long as I can remember, but I don't. I can't. Instead, I say, "You talk big, Darla, for someone who's not allowed to even car date yet."

We both laugh enjoying the warmth of the night and the lights along 97.

The next day, when Mama and I return to the house, there are whiskey bottles strewn amongst the normal rubble, a pair of panties is in the trash pile, and the cigarette smoke clings to everything like a cloud of death. "Looks like Dad had a goddam helluva party."

"Doncha talk like that, Sandy. God'll punish you for takin' His name in vain," Mama warns.

"He's got cause to punish me for more than that, Mama."

"Hush up, don't be talkin' to your Mama like that."

I shake my head and start opening windows to get the stench out. I toss the panties into a trash can and cover them over with the whiskey bottles.

Someone starts pounding on the door.

"Hold your horses," Mama yells out. "I'm comin'."

When she opens the door, she says, "George Jenkins, what are you doing here? You look like the hair of the dog. You best be gettin' home to that wife of your'n."

"Where's Al? I need to talk to Al." George strides into the room. His eyes are bloodshot and he reeks of day-old boozing.

"Like Mama says, Dad's not here."

"I'll wait." George plops down on the sofa and rubs his eyes like he can force the redness away.

A short time later I hear Dad's car rolling over the gravel outside. George grasps his hands together twisting them so hard they turn red. His eyes stare expectantly at the door. When Al steps in, George stands up, gripping his fists to his side.

"George, what the hell are you doing here?"

George just stares at Al.

"Mama, take Sandy and get in the bedroom. I gotta talk with George here."

I follow Mama back and shut the door to, leaving a crack to hear through.

"Big Al, did you take care of it?" It is emphasized with a hard T.

"Stop worrying. It's taken care of."

"Where did you bury them?"

George's voice is high pitch and every word carries like he's speaking into a megaphone.

"Keep it down, George. Haven't you caused enough trouble? You want me to plow you under in the Deschutes River Woods, too?"

"We shouldn't have gotten so carried away, Al."

"Your son found the girls and brought them here, George. You and your wife were having a real humping time with that little redheaded gal."

"Don't bring that up, not now. It was a mistake. A big mistake, Al."

Their voices are getting louder. They won't hear me crack the door a bit more. I ease out into the narrow hall so I can see. Mama whispers. "Get back in here, Sandy. Some things're better not knowing." I ignore her.

"Look here, George," Dad says as he lifts George up by his shirt collar. "You didn't complain about banging a little ass last night, did you? You shoulda thought of that when you drugged their drinks."

"You're right, Al. You're right," George says. He groans when Dad loosens his grip. "Listen, I told my son that we woke the girls up after he left. You'll back me on that, won't you?"

"Why not? Anyway, they were hitchhikers. Nobody'll miss 'em and take my word for it, George, nobody'll find 'em. Now get on home."

"Okay, Al. Okay."

George flees. Dad starts laughing as soon as the front door closes.

I back against the wall and through the bedroom door. My hands are ice cold and a shiver runs through my body. When I look at Mama, her eyes are wide with fear and something else, maybe sorrow.

CHAPTER FOURTEEN

"Who's that heading up our road?" Dad asks as he peers through the front door.

The tan sedan creeps slowly toward the house. Dad fondles the gun in the front of his work pants.

"Wait, Dad, I'll go see," I say stepping in front of Dad and off the front stoop.

As I get closer to the car, a man leans his bald head out the window. When he takes off his sunglasses, I start. It's my school principal, Mr. Hayward.

"Hi, there, Sandy," he says as he opens his car door and steps out. "I've been worried about you. You've missed a lot of school."

I swallow hard, not sure what to say, and real surprised that anyone from school even noticed. What can I say, that my dad needed me for his business? What then? Explain that his business is robbing houses?

"I've been busy, taking care of my grandmother. She's been real sick."

"Sorry about your grandmother, Sandy, but school's important, too. Can't someone else in the family help out?" Mr. Hayward's question hangs there awhile. I try to think up an answer.

Before I have a chance to speak, I hear Dad's work boots clomping across the gravel drive. "Just who might you be?" he asks.

Mr. Hayward's at least two heads shorter than Dad. He shields his eyes from the September sun and says, "I'm Mr. Hayward, the principal, from Sandy's school."

"So why aren't you there taking care of your job instead of here interfering with me and mine?" Dad's question has a harsh edge to it.

I can see Mr. Hayward's Adam's apple jump up and down as he wipes his hands on his dress pants. "Sandy is one of my pupils and, frankly, I've been worried about her. She's missed more days than she's been there."

"Well, Mr. Hayward, is it? You're meddling in my family business here. I suggest, and I hope there is no misunderstanding, that you just get right back in your car there and tend to your other pupils."

Mr. Hayward nods at my dad and scurries to his car. I want to shout out to him, don't leave. Come back, but dust swirls behind the sedan's back wheels as he burns rubber.

"Sandy, you get on back inside. No more school for you. You've graduated."

"But, Dad, I like school. I…"

"Enough, girl. Get inside." Dad lights another cigarette and stares toward the roadway.

A few days later, Dad comes home and tosses a set of keys on the kitchen table.

"It's about time we had a place of our own, way out of town and out of the sneaky eyes of people who can't mind their own business."

"Where?" Mama asks with her own brand of resignation in the tone.

"Bend. Out in the valley. Close to Molly and Paul, but not too close. Right nice spot. Part of the house is built, the other part framed."

When my dad drives us to our new place, we pass by a pond circled by tall lodgepole pines. They're so green that they make the sky look bluer.

"What's this called?" I ask.

"Deschutes River Woods," he answers.

A shudder crosses my shoulder blades when I think about those two girls who are supposed to be buried there. I sneak a look back at Mama. We hold our gaze and our tongues.

"We're almost there," Dad says a few minutes later.

When we drive down the dirt road, I can see the framing of a couple of rooms. They look like skeletons against the valley.

"I'll be a sonuva bitch," Dad says. "They've moved the finished part of the house away."

"Do something, son. We cain't live there." Mama clutches her sweater around her.

Dad turns around in his seat, his cigarette dangles in his mouth and barely moves when he says, "You'll live where I say you'll live."

Mama and I tack sheets around the framing. Dad nails a few pieces of plywood on the north side to keep out the worst of the wind.

In the night when the wind howls, the sheets ripple and billow. When they snap, I cling to Mama. Wind has followed me from back porches to tin box trailers. I hate the sound of it, the feel of it on my skin.

A couple of my cousins and an uncle join us at the house. It's good having company and to hear the sound of hammers building a real shelter. Dad is gone on a construction job during the week and I feel free to laugh and joke with Frankie, Joey, and Uncle Calvin.

One day at the grocery store, I hear a man talking behind me. "Yeah, I think you're right. There's a bunch of hippies down in the valley. Hope it's not one of those crazy commune things."

Us, they're talking about us. Hippie Valley. That'll give Dad a laugh.

On weekends, Dad takes pleasure in teaching his trade to the others in the family. We cut quite a swathe through the Columbia Valley. We must have hit twenty houses that fall.

Mama couldn't seem to get warm at the ramshackle house. It was colder than a witch's tit, she said. Mama could abide a lot, but not any more freezing weather.

"Come, Sandy girl. I gotta plan," she says to me.

She leads the way into the welfare office and stomps right up to the desk.

"I got a bad heart," she announces in a loud voice. "This here's my granddaughter. She's been takin' care of me nigh onto a year."

Mama slowly sits down in the molded plastic chair. I can hear her knees creak as she gingerly stretches them out in front of her.

"What do you want me to do, ma'am?" the gentle-voiced lady asks. She leans forward over her scarred metal desk and her black hair glides toward her bent nose. I guess she's about fifty or so.

"I need a warm place to live. Somewhere safe and some place with an inside toilet. My hips be hurtin' too much to be wadin' knee-deep in snow."

Mama props her clasped hands on her oversized vinyl pocket book and stares at the lady whose eyes have widened in a look of wonder. By the time we leave, Mama has a promise of an apartment in a low income housing project. The welfare worker says that I will be getting some money to look after Mama.

Mama is very pleased with herself. She says, "Well, baby, we're getting out of Hippie Valley and your daddy ain't gonna know about that little bit of money you'll be gettin', do ya hear? He takes my social security widow's check. Papa's probably turning in his grave. God rest his soul. He takes the welfare checks. I reckon he's getting checks from both Oregon and California, but I cain't swear to it."

A month later, while Dad's on a construction job, Mama and I pile our sheets and blankets, assorted pots and pan, and our clothes into the car. Joey helps me tie the mattress to the top and to fit Mama's wooden rocker in the back seat.

"You sure you should be doin' this?" he asks. He has that worried look people get when they think about Big Al.

"Don't worry your mind, Joey. Help an old lady into this here car."

Joey opens the door, hugs Mama, and waves a good-bye to us.

The apartments are noisy. A lot of little kids run up and down the outside stairs. We can hear neighbors yelling across at each other and husbands and wives arguing behind the thin walls.

Mama grins at me as she walks back and forth across the living room to the kitchen.

"Don't that paint smell good? A real stove, not that old wood stove I've been puttin' up with. Sandy, set my rocker right here. Right in the middle of the floor."

After I set it down, Mama sighs and eases herself in. She rocks back and forth, humming to herself. Then she stares up at the light fixture.

"Turn on the light, Sandy. No more oil lamps for a while."

After I flip the switch, she rocks back and forth in a slow peaceful motion. "Remember, child, in that old house when the ceiling caved in on me?"

"I sure do, Mama. You just sat in the chair and kept rocking. The plaster was falling all around you and you were covered in white dust. You looked like a ghost, rocking and singing."

"That landlady fixed that place up fast-like, didn't she?"

"Probably had something to do with your looking crazy and threatening to sue."

"Didn't even have to have one of my heart attacks, did I?"

While Mama rocks contentedly, I run water in the bathtub. Steam rises up warm as a summer night, frosting the mirror and blocking the glare of the overhead bulb. I sink into the porcelain tub letting the water roll over me like a million caressing hands. When I move my arms about like fan blades, waves swoop around me, lapping away yesterday's cold and the blustery anger of the winter winds.

CHAPTER FIFTEEN

The overpowering scent of Old Spice wafts through the screen door. I know from the footsteps before I answer the persistent knocking that it's my dad. He has his hair slicked back but some strands overhang his ears, a feeble attempt to hide their size. It looks like he's wearing a new shirt, as if he wants to impress Mama and me.

"Unlatch this screen door, Sandy, and give your daddy a big hug," he says with the honeyed smoothness he uses with waitresses and anyone else he wants to persuade to do something.

Behind him, I see Dianne who lives on the floor above us.

"Sandy, look who I brought to see you. I ran into him in the parking lot. He looked so lost that I knew he needed rescuing," Dianne says as she smiles up at my dad. "You two enjoy your visit. Nice to meetcha, Al."

Dad watches Dianne walk away and up the stairs. I notice she's added a bit more hip action than normal.

Once in the room, Dad says, "Where's the old lady?"

"Sleeping." I stand beside the screen door, as if being near the open air, I'll be safe.

"Nice place here. Did you think I wouldn't find you?" His eyes are slitted while he questions me. I turn my head aside and look across the parking lot toward the open park area. I wish I were there now swinging high with my legs pushing through the breeze.

"I knew you'd be here soon enough. It's only been two days."

"Well, you and your grandmother did okay with this place. Not to my taste, right in the middle of town. Nice neighbor lady though. What's her name again?" Dad moves toward Mama's rocking chair and gives it a push. It creaks and moans without Mama in it.

"Dianne."

"Does Dianne have children?"

"Two," I say. Dad's eyes question me. I answer, "a boy four and a girl seven."

"Might just get to know that Dianne. Yessir, think I'll settle in with you and Mama a while."

That next night Dianne, Mama, Dad, and I are sitting at the picnic table by the play area.

"I can't believe I have to work a double shift tomorrow," Dianne says. "Nursing homes are always understaffed."

"I'll watch your babies for you," Dad offers.

"Thanks, Al, but I can call a sitter. I'm sure you have a girlfriend to see or something," Dianne says with an underlying question in her voice.

"No. No girlfriend, not yet," he says. He smiles wide and Dianne blushes. "I'd be glad to help you out with your kids. Save you some money besides."

"Are you sure?"

"Hey, listen, I can babysit, Dianne," I interrupt. "I'm crazy about your kids. Mama is, too."

"Next time, Sandy. How else can I get into Dianne's good graces?" Dad asks.

"You're already in my good graces, Al."

"So what time will you need me…to sit?" Dad asks.

"I go in at three this afternoon and won't be home till morning. Are you sure you won't mind being with those two all night?"

Dad smiles and shakes his head.

My throat tightens so hard I'm not sure I can swallow. Dad alone for hours with a little girl. He always manages to find the women with children. He sweet talks, he fills them with fantasies of the perfect man for their children, and he leaves later having shattered hearts and damaged souls. He abused me, Jolene, my cousins, my mother, and who knows how many others? Is there a special place in hell for my dad?

"Sandy, are you still with us?" Dianne asks as she waves her hand in front of my eyes. "Do you want to come up for ice cream at my place?"

"Sandy has some work to do, don't you, honey?" Dad's question requires no response, so I walk back to the apartment with Mama in tow.

I hear Dianne's laughter as she leads my father upstairs and into her life.

As the days go by, I have seen her daughter Tammy walking hand in hand with my dad. On the playground swing, she sits on his lap as he swings them forward and back. Tammy still smiles readily. How soon before the smiles are slow in coming and her eyes hold the vacant stare of defeat?

Friday morning arrives with a dusting of snow. By noon the mountain sun has melted it away. Dad decides we should go ahead with business as usual. The trip across the Washington line is fruitful. We rob a house ripe for the picking, as Dad says. He laughs at his own joke since the house is located in wine country.

The crystal is packed carefully between damask tablecloths, lace and needlepoint napkins. A walnut chest held twelve place settings of sterling silver. As a bonus, Dad had found a gun collection and a shimmering sword. A porcelain clock was cradled in layers of silk undergarments.

Exhaustion claims me as it usually does after a robbery. The fear, the excitement, and the adventure all mix together. Only sleep can give me the distance I crave.

Night sounds, passing cars, Mama's snores, and the click of my dad's Zippo lighter, remind me that I am still traveling toward home. Through half shut eyes I watch the headlights flickering like armies of lightning bugs.

"I know you're awake, girly girl. Come over here next to your daddy."

I mumble and change positions as if I'm still asleep struggling to wake up.

The side door panel offers a cushiony reprieve.

"Sit up. Look out there. See how the rich bitches live," Dad says. The end of his lighted cigarette reflects in the windshield and swirls glowing red with his gesture.

Beside us is a mown pasture with trees and small ponds. The golf course stretches a mile down the road. Up ahead to the right is a lighted driveway leading to the country club. I imagine women wearing velvet dresses, mink coats, and diamonds, as they hold the arms of dashing men in fitted tuxedos.

The dreamy mood ends when I see the Cadillac easing onto the roadway ahead of us. Dad doesn't see the car. His foot never leaves the accelerator. I scream. Too late.

We crash into the car broadside. The driver's side waffles on impact then the car rolls over and over like a wayward wagon wheel. Inside the passengers are tousled like rag dolls.

Our Mercury station wagon stalls. My arms are wrenched from bracing against the dashboard. Mama lies crumpled on the back floorboard. Her moans are at least a sign of life.

"Sonuva bitch. Sonuva bitch," Dad says over and over as he tries to restart the car.

"Shouldn't we stop? Those people must be hurt," I say staring at the demolished car.

Dad ignores me as he turns the ignition again. The motor purrs to life and the car lurches forward. Dad's eyes focus straight ahead. He veers off on a side road bypassing the flashing lights rolling toward us.

Once in town he parks on a side street. Dad tells us to stay put and sets out on foot. The glow of his cigarette is the last thing I see for the better part of an hour.

I crawl over and help Mama roll back onto the seat. I massage her legs that are aching from the fall. She moans as her arthritic hips throb.

"Did we kill someone?" she asks. "How bad was it?"

"Bad, Mama. Real bad."

When Dad comes back, we drive in silence. Dad parks in the middle of the apartment lot and I help him carry the packed suitcases back to the house. Mama stumbles against me and muffles her low groans.

Inside the apartment, Mama topples onto the bed. When I slide the quilt onto her, she cries out.

"No, baby. It's too heavy. Let me be. Let me be."

Dad is unpacking the crystal from the tablecloth and napkins. The kitchen table glitters as the light shines on the cut glass. A flickering shadow plays on the walls.

"It's fine. Just fine. Not a scratch."

The porcelain clock is already resting on the kitchen counter.

"That stupid peckerwood had so much money he thought he'd live forever. His car crumpled like cheap paper. Battle Creek, helluva name for a country club. He sure as hell lost his battle."

CHAPTER SIXTEEN

"I can't believe how lucky you are, Sandy. This car is so cool," Darla says.

The Olds Cutlass peels out from the stoplight as if it's traveling on a thunderbolt. Beside us, a carload of guys shout and whistle. I ignore them pretending I'm not interested. Darla is waving and giggling. For fourteen, we think we're pretty neat.

Life is sweet when I'm rumbling down 97, holding the power under my bare foot. The ripples on the accelerator tickle my arch. The excitement of the chase tickles my imagination.

As we idle at a stoplight, a jacked-up Chevy roars next to us. I know the guy is wrestling to keep the car from bolting away.

"Hey, hot stuff. Wanta race?" the driver calls out to me over the rumble of the engines.

The other boys in the car call jabs and dares. They are laughing at me, at the idea of racing, and at the foolishness of youth.

"What are the stakes?" I ask with my confidence billowing.

Darla is telling me to shut up. She asks me if I'm crazy. It must be your time of the month, she suggests.

"A roll in the hay?" the driver yells back.

"That does nothing for me," I say.

The other guys hoot with laughter. One shrieks that I'm a ball buster. Another adds that a good lay is what I need.

I'm thinking that boys are so juvenile. Darla is spouting off at me about losing my marbles.

We crawl down the street side by side. Again the driver makes an offer, ten dollars.

"What a wimp bet. Title or nothing," I say.

Darla warns me that I've lost my mind. "Men in white coats are gonna take you away," she says. "Don't do it, Sandy. This car is so cool."

"Title or nothing," I challenge him again. I can hear the other boys egging him on. You gonna let some pussy scare you off, one says. Yeah, yeah, the others agree.

He nods. I follow him to a stretch of dirt road outside of town. The car purrs under me, vibrations keeping rhythm with my galloping heart.

We line up side-by-side. One of the boys gets out of the Chevy and walks a few paces down the road. I am intent on his hand that's raised high in the air. As it falls, I bury my foot on the accelerator. My toes grip it; feeling the power of the engine surge through my body.

My hair flies as we careen neck and neck down the pitted dirt road. I let him keep pace with me for a moment. Darla is arched with her foot pressing the floorboard. Fear shines in her eyes.

Then, I free the Olds and we shoot forward. Every second thrusts into another. The speedometer edges up and up. The Olds roars. The arrow slides past 100. Like a stallion, the car gallops over ruts and gravel. Dust shadows behind us with the Chevy in our wake.

The tree boundary marks the finish line and I ease up on the accelerator. The Olds purrs back to its cruising speed. I ease the brake down and cut left, blocking the roadway and waiting for the Chevy to catch up.

Darla takes a deep breath and releases her imaginary brake pedal.

"You burned up the road. You beat his ass."

"Not so crazy, huh?"

"I didn't say that. You're still crazy. Cool, but crazy."

Standing beside my midnight-blue stallion, I have one foot on the dirt road and the other on the running board. I drape my arm over the car door.

The Chevy driver is slumped over his steering wheel. From the catcalls inside his car, I can tell he's taken a lot of heat for losing to a girl.

"Let's go to your house for the title," I say. "I can follow you."

"Are you for real? I didn't agree to no race for titles." There is a shrillness to his voice. The kind of shrillness that comes from the strain of lying.

"I have plenty of witnesses. Don't I, boys?"

The driver whips his car around and lurches away from me and the smile that's eating a hole in my face. The story will be all over town tomorrow. The next challenge won't be taken lightly. The next challenge will bring me a car title.

The following afternoon, Dad comes home from work boiling mad. "What the hell are you thinking racing around like that? You want to get every cop in the county on our case?"

"Nobody's gonna be on my case except, of course, the guys who lose their titles to me."

"You're getting a smart mouth, girl."

"I'm paying for this car fair and square. You made the deal, remember?"

"You best remember you're working it out in trade. I still got twenty times coming before this baby is paid off. That's twenty more rolls in the hay."

He'd been sticking it to me for nothing since I was six. At least now I had something to show for it.

Months later I had title to a souped up '69 Thunderbird.

"Your daddy gives you everything you want. Wish my dad was like yours," Darla says when we're sitting at A&W.

"No, you don't, Darla," I say. The froth from the root beer soothes the aching in my throat.

"You know you're getting a big rep as a hot rodder. Everybody's talking about Blondie. That's such a cool CB handle. Wish I had a handle. Hell, wish I had a CB," Darla says. I can hear the envy in her voice.

"What's your mom saying about my big rep? One of her cop friends could put an end to your riding shotgun."

"Mom thinks Blondie is some older girl. Her working graveyard shift keeps us out of each other's way." Darla groans and says, "Thank goodness. I'd be grounded until I'm out high school."

We sit quietly, watching the other kids circulating from car to car. An older guy, maybe twenty-two or so, is looking over at us. His light brown hair waves over his forehead. He calls one of the carhops over and points at my car. They laugh together a moment. When he backs out of the lot, he smiles at me and tips his head a bit.

That's what I want, I say to myself. A man. Not one of these little boys who follow me around like dogs in heat. When the carhop comes over to remove the tray, I ask her who was asking about me?

"Oh, that was Pete. He was admiring your wheels," she says.

"Is he from around here?"

"Yeah, works at some auto parts store. Some kind of manager."

Pete, nice name, I think to myself. Nice smile, too. Maybe I'll need to buy some spark plugs sometime soon.

Plans to check out Pete in the auto parts store were detoured by Dad's insistence on upping the burglary pace. We hit houses in northern California, western Oregon, and on both sides of the Cascades in Washington. One strip of homes, near the Columbia River Gorge, we hit twice in a few months.

Dad prides himself on his ability to find every back road and every accessible escape route. He has a backwoodsman sense of location which he proves by the mounting numbers of successful jobs he's done without being caught or apprehended.

"I'm never going back to prison. My real dad died in the Joint. Hell, he was younger than I am now. If you can't be king of the hill, you got no business being there."

Dad's either darn lucky or he has a guardian angel. Mama once said he had friends in important places. I wonder what she means, but I dare not ask. She won't tell me anything about her Al. "What you don't know can't hurt you," she says.

The few times that the house has been raided by the police or FBI, Dad has a phone call beforehand. He manages to hide the loot. Once he even stored a stash of guns and jewels under Klamath Falls. The guns were a mess when he retrieved the plastic bag, but the jewelry was only slightly tarnished. Who warns Dad? Who does Dad meet out at the mile marker?

Tonight I'm standing guard at a house in the Tri-Cities. "A car's pulling up the driveway," I call out to Dad who's lugging a bag of pewter candlesticks and mugs. I follow him out the back and we circle around about a half mile. He hides the bag in a cluster of bushes and we head away from the house through a back pasture to another road. We walk beside it near the irrigation ditch. When headlights approach, we slide into the ditch. The mud clings to my jacket and I slide deeper into the slippery undergrowth.

I can hear sirens in the distance. Across from the hidden clearing, we can see the lights flashing outside the house we just robbed. When we get to the car, Dad tells me to drive. Slowly I ease out of the cluster of trees, careful not to raise any dirt clouds. My night vision is better than Dad's now so I can drive further without the headlights on. Once we're on the state highway, I turn on the beams and force myself to stick to the speed limit.

A car is gaining on us. All of a sudden red lights are twirling.

"Sonuva bitch. He's not gonna pass. He wants us to pull over. Let's move it."

With all the power hidden beneath the hood of the battered sedan, I am able to shoot ahead. 'Smokey's' still back there, holding in, but not catching up.

"It'll be four lanes soon," Dad says. "Get on your CB. Need some cover-up and fast."

"Breaker, breaker, this is Blondie, do you copy? Need some cover. Smokey in pursuit."

"Come ahead, little lady. We'll take the heat off."

I let the car out full throttle and shoot ahead to the semis I could see ahead. I dart between them and slow to their pace. As the siren screeches louder and louder, I jerk onto the right shoulder, the trucks cover the distance and I ramble next to them until Smokey bursts ahead.

Again I move between them, I wave my thanks as I turn onto a secluded side road.

"Right good job, Blondie. You've had such a good teacher," Dad says sliding closer to me. "I still got a lesson or two to teach you."

I ease up on the gas and pull to the side of the road. "Thanks, Dad. I am whipped and appreciate your taking the wheel."

As I'm walking around the car to the passenger door, Dad is shaking his head. When I get back in, he lets me sleep the rest of the way home. Next weekend we will head back to the pasture and retrieve the bag of pewter. He'll probably want to hit the house again. We had to rush out so fast. Dad doesn't like getting interrupted.

CHAPTER SEVENTEEN

"Come on, Sandy. It'll be a great party. Loreen's parents will be gone and everything," Darla says. "Say you'll come, please."

"I'm busy Friday night, Darla. You know that weekends are family time at my house," I say.

We're sitting in the K-Mart parking lot. Darla's stealing a smoke before she goes home. I'm watching her try to French inhale and the smoke is not cooperating.

The radio's playing Diana Ross. She's singing about romance and love. Touch me in the morning she croons in her sultry and sexy voice. Dad would say she's just another cock-teaser.

"Can't you get away just one Friday night? Your family's so tight you probably all go to the john together." Darla laughs and I laugh with her thinking she's more on target than she can imagine.

That night, as I lay next to Mama watching the water spot that's creeping down the bedroom wall, I can feel the burning in my stomach. I feel like a prisoner allowed out to the exercise yard and then forced to work at my prison job. Afterwards, I am closed in my cell for safekeeping.

Just then I hear the scratching on the window screen. My stomach fire scalds more deeply as if acid is seeping through my whole system. My jailer waits outside as I slip on my jeans and tiptoe out to join him in the back of his white van.

Lying there in the darkness I stare at the stained metal roof while Dad fondles, tweaks, and pummels me. I think of Darla, parties I can't go to, boyfriends that are forbidden, and life away from Bear Creek Road. The blaze in my belly becomes a wildfire as I plan my escape.

A few days later, Dad says he'll be home early afternoon. He orders me to prepare the burglary kit and fill the gasoline cans. I intend to prepare a lot more.

After I've finished Dad's list and my own personal plan, it's mid-afternoon.

"Come on, Mama. Let's pretend we're Southern ladies, drink iced tea, and watch the world go by," I say as I tote her rocking chair into the side yard next to the petunias she's planted.

Tinker follows along behind us, his three legs moving in their own makeshift way. I throw a blanket onto the weeds and plop down beside her.

"Nothing so great about Southern ladies. Don't know what puts such notions in your head. My own mama wuz a Southern lady and she got herself poisoned by her older brother. After they threw her in the lake, they sent me and my brother from pillar to post. Slaves that's what we wuz," Mama says right before she does her snorty harrumph.

Before I can respond to Mama, Dad's van pulls in front of the trailer. My heart starts racing and pounding harder than my car speakers on bass. Mama starts to get up.

"Stay put," I say as I pat her arm. "He'll find us soon enough."

I ease around the side of the trailer and watch Dad, cigarette in mouth, pull open the trailer door. I hear a whooshing sound and a cloud of flame blows out. Dad leaps backward tripping down the wooden stairs. He lands on his feet, spits the cigarette from his mouth, and brushes his face with an open palm.

He disappears behind the trailer toward the propane tanks and then returns to the side yard. "What the hell did you do that for?" he asks me. I stare back, but the flame didn't even singe his eyebrows.

"Best be going, Sandy. We got work to do. Think we'll head over to Sacramento. Haven't done any jobs there in a while. Come on, old lady. You're coming with."

"Sandy, get the kit from the trailer and bring something for us to eat while we're on the road." His eyes are shining. He knows I'm scared to death to go in the trailer.

When I hit the door, the rancid odor of propane gas greets me. I grab the kit from the table and pull a quart of buttermilk from the fridge. I snatch some soda crackers and peanut butter and run like hell out of the trailer, slamming the door behind me.

Dad laughs his low belly guffaws and Mama stares at him quizzical-like. She hadn't heard the whoosh or seen the fire cloud. She had rocked and hummed through the whole thing.

In Sacramento, hours later, Dad and I stand in the living room of the latest soon-to-be burgled house. Dad grins and whispers, "Lookee here. A white couch just like Mama wants. Guess lady luck is with us."

I groan. "Dad, the van's a mile away."

"So?" he says. "We'll get the suitcases back there first then come back for the couch."

"It's ugly though," I say. It looks like it's made out of plastic go-go boots. "White's white."

Mama's excited when we tell her we're going back for the couch. "Cain't ya drive a little closer, son. That's a hard haul for Sandy."

"Won't hurt her any. Besides she owes me after the stunt she pulled today."

As we haul the couch across the field, I think my arms are going to come right out of their sockets. My shoulders burn and ache. The upholstery tacks at the bottom pierce holes in the palm of my hand.

The couch gets heavier and heavier. The thicket of trees where the car is hidden looks miles away. My breath comes in sharp gasps by the time we lift the monster couch into the back of the van.

The next morning when we unload it, I start to laugh. The daylight shows the couch's true color, a bright yellow. It looks like a kid mixed green and yellow crayons together and painted it. Mama loves the squishing, whooshing sound it makes when she eases into it. Dad calls it her whoopee cushion.

Dad and Mama like living outside the city. Mama plants her rose bushes and pots of flowers beside the house or trailer, wherever they happen to be living. Mama never takes care of the inside of the house. Sometimes I think we move because so much junk stacks up that Mama wants to start over.

"Al, go check on the piglets," Mama says after supper. "Didn't have time to slop their mama this morning."

"Come on, honey. Take a walk with your daddy."

While we're watching the piglets suckle, a man walks up the gravel road toward us. He's not much taller than me, about five-six, but he's built strongly, muscles rippling through his tee shirt. His hair's dark and his olive skin's clean-shaven.

"Nice evening," he says.

"Right nice," Dad says.

They make conversation. The man's name is Tony and he just moved down the lane with his wife and brood of kids.

"Lot of family to take care of," Dad says.

"Yeah, keeping them in shoes and clothes costs a fortune these days."

"Some guys find easier ways to make money than taking a pail to the plant," Dad says.

"Like that bicycle bandit? He kept those cops running in circles for months," Tony says chuckling. He shakes his head and looks Dad straight in the eye. "The cops woulda never caught him if his girlfriend hadn't of ratted him out."

"How much was his take?" Dad asks staring right back.

As I watch them, I think they're saying more than they're saying, almost like two fighters sizing each other up. Dad's six-foot-five frame towers over Tony, but the man doesn't flinch when he looks up at my dad.

"Enough," Tony answers. "I coulda used some of it."

Dad nods and says, "I know what you mean."

"Well, I better get on home. Nice talking to you, Al, and meeting you, young lady."

"Come by for a beer one night and we'll talk some more," Dad says.

Dad watches Tony walk away. When Tony turns toward the other street, he turns and waves.

"You think he'll really come over?" I ask.

"Sure. He knows the score. Yessir, we might even be doing business together."

CHAPTER EIGHTEEN

Tony likes to come by and visit. He teases Mama about her CB radio and me about being fifteen and never been kissed. Dad and Tony started doing jobs together several months ago and as Dad says it's been right profitable.

"Granny," Tony says to Mama. "You have a good heart. You keep those truckers laughing."

He calls Mama 'Granny,' like she's his own grandma. Since she started talking on the CB, she keeps herself occupied chatting with the truckers.

"Some handle," Tony says. "Granny-in-the-Woods. Can you beat that?"

Tony scrunches down in the plastic couch cushions and holds his beer on his knee. Dad still wearing his hard hat sits at the kitchen table with his leg propped up. Mama's rocking with Tinker in her lap. I'm sitting at the other end of the couch, a Pepsi propped on the couch arm. If anybody walked in, I think, they'd never guess we're a house of thieves.

"I sure getta kick out of your daddy. He lugged that Caterpillar battery off like it was a box of corn flakes."

Dad tipped his hat at Tony's compliment.

"Must say though I'd never hire you at my construction site."

"I give 'em fair and square labor. Support my union, cover their asses with the inspectors, and collect my paycheck," Dad says adding, "then I rob 'em blind when the job's over."

"Like I said, wouldn't hire you on my construction site."

The mood is light. The six clocks chiming on the hour don't even bother me. I'm planning my getaway. Dad and Tony are pulling a heist tonight. A score I'm not in on. I'm pulling my own job, I'm running away, as soon as they take off.

Finally, Mama's sleeping soundly, flat on her back to spare the pain in her hips, with the covers up to her chin. I slip a few clothes in a duffel bag, steal some cash from my dad's stash in one of his coffee cans, and head out to my T-bird. When thoughts of the buried girls and the dead prisoners flicker into my mind, I shut the ideas away. As far as I know, Dad's never killed kinfolk. Fear flashes through me like a lightening bolt before it submerges and hides with my other secrets.

Besides, Loreen's waiting for me at her place. Dad doesn't know Loreen or any of my other friends so I will stay with her a while until I figure out what to do.

As I drive down highway 20 to Sisters, a sense of freedom makes me light-headed. I want to shout at everyone on the highway that I'm free, white, and fifteen. A disco beat vibrates my car and I tap my fingers on the steering wheel. I know Dad's gonna be mad as hell when he figures it out. Mama'll be worried sick, but I'll call her tomorrow. Tonight I'm going to a party, a real party on a Saturday night.

When Loreen, Darla, and I drive up to Dave's house, the lights are low and the music is loud. There are at least fifteen cars parked up and down the street. I spot one couple draped over a car hood going at it like no one can see.

"I wonder what kind of action is going on *inside*," Darla says. Loreen rolls her eyes then pats her nose with powder. Her lipstick is a shocking pink which glares next to her red hair.

"If your sweater was much tighter, Sandy, I'd guess it was painted on," Darla teases. She's flat chested and has out-and-out said she's jealous as hell. I don't say that my dad likes me to dress like this. The more I look like one of his whores the better. Still, I have to confess I don't mind boys eyeing me.

When we walk in, I can feel the boys sizing us up like we're prime cattle ready for slaughter. Billy Joe calls out to Loreen, "Over here, you sweet thing." Loreen struts to him, pleased to be singled out. I think Billy Joe needs a face transplant, he has so many pimples, but Loreen's crazy about him and his souped up car.

"Looks like a dead group," Darla whispers to me. "I need some passion punch then I'll liven the place up."

After pulling a cold beer from a washtub filled with ice, I spot an empty chair and drift toward it. I never drink anybody's house drinks. Never know what might be in it. Darla trusts everyone and I trust no one. One gawky kid tries to make eye contact. I turn my head away.

As more and more punch is downed, the party starts swinging. Loreen and Billy Joe are dancing so close they look hooked together at the hip. Darla dances in the center of the room, rotating her hips and swishing her long hair back and forth. Several boys have taken an interest and are sniffing around her like stallions in mating season.

As I watch, I feel so separated from these kids. I don't fit. I don't like their games. I think I'll head out for games of my own. Highway 97 beckons.

As I cruise up and down, I see a few carloads of drunk kids probably heading to another party. One guy revs his engine at the stoplight, but I know he's no challenge. At the A&W I splurge on a root beer float, after all, it's Dad's money.

While I'm spooning the vanilla ice cream out of the mug, I figure Tony and Dad are stealing enough to more than make up for the dollars I lifted. A car angles in behind, blocking me. The headlights glare in my rearview mirror. What if Dad's found me already? I've only been gone a few hours. My shoulders slump and I have a sinking feeling sucking out my energy.

"Hi, you're in my favorite spot," the voice says. Startled I look across the car tray into a stranger's face. "Sorry, didn't mean to scare you."

"Well, you did," I say, trying to act grown-up because I definitely want to impress this man. His light brown hair scruffs down over a handsome face. His voice is deep and warm.

"Nice car," he says. "I hear you handle it well, too."

"Thanks, I like driving."

"I hear you like racing."

While he talks about RPM and manifolds, I notice the cute way his lips edge over his even teeth. I interject a few nods and a word or two. Mostly, I think how I'd like to tousle his hair and kiss him.

"Up for a spin in my car?" he asks.

"I don't even know your name," I say.

"Pete. Pete Keaton. I work right around the corner."

Then I remember seeing him before. Was it a year ago?

"I'm Sandy."

"I know who you are. I like your nickname, Blondie. Mind if I call you Blondie?" his smile lights up his eyes like firecrackers and I'm lost in their flame for a minute. I consider saying, 'you can call me anything,' but I stop myself.

"How about it, Blondie? A short spin?"

"What if I say no?" I ask.

"I'll stay parked behind you until you agree or until I have to show up for work whichever comes first."

"Then I guess the answer's yes."

Pete backs out and I park my car at the abandoned gas station nearby. He opens the door for me and makes a sweeping bow. Have I met my knight in shining armor?

As we drive down 97, I feel strange. I'm not in the driver's seat. I'm an observer listening to the rev of the engine and unable to test the accelerator.

When Pete drops me at my car, he says, "Next time, you can take me for a spin."

He opens my car door for me and leans toward me. His aftershave is a bold scent nothing like Dad's Old Spice. "When will next time be?" he asks.

"I'm not sure yet. I'm just getting settled in a new place."

"Can I have your phone number?" he asks.

"Too soon to be giving out my number to a stranger," I say laughing.

"You know where to find me. Come by the store."

As I drive away, I wave and smile. Some things have to be on my own terms. Still, the scent of his aftershave lingers.

I wait a week before I go by Pete's. He's behind the auto parts service counter and welcomes me with a broad smile. A plastic badge saying assistant manager is pinned to his gray shirt.

"Didn't know you were such an important man," I say.

Pete flushes, before saying, "Hey, I have a dinner break in an hour. Want to pick me up out front?"

"Sure, why not?" I sway my hips slightly when I walk away and one of the men turns to stare at me. I like being blonde and a little curvy. It makes for an easier life sometimes.

A week later Loreen comes to the back bedroom and says, "Someone's here to see you and I don't think you're going to like it."

Dad, I thought. He's found me.

Dad dwarfs the small living room. He's holding his hard hat in his hand and his fingers are gripped so tightly they're turning white. "Get your clothes. Get in your car. I'm following you home."

Once we're back at the trailer, he lights into me. "Hear you've been whoring around with some guy in town. Is that so?"

"I'm dating him. Not whoring around."

Mama says, "Stop talking like that about Sandy."

"Mind your own business, you old cow. Sandy's been seen cuddling up with some guy and driving up and down the main drag. That's whoring in my book." Dad doesn't raise his voice, but there's no mistaking there's hell to pay.

"Fornicatin' before marriage be a sin, but my baby ain't doing that." Mama rocks faster in her chair and wrings her hands.

"There's plenty you don't know about what goes on, old lady." There's a threat in his voice and he looks at me. He knows the truth would kill Mama and he knows I know.

Later that night, Dad says he's taking me out for ice cream. Mama nods, pats Tinker, and turns on her CB. "You be careful with that CB. You better watch what you're saying and who you're saying it to. Some things are family business and in this family, we keep quiet around strangers."

As Dad drives down the dirt road away from town, I know we're not getting ice cream. I can't jump out. As usual, the passenger door handle is missing and the vise grip that's usually under the seat to open it isn't there. The back of the van stinks of sex and fear. After Dad finishes with me, he holds my arms down over my head and says, "You don't give this out to anyone unless I say so. That punk you're seeing could disappear just like that guy did in Salem."

With Dad glaring down at me, his breath reeks of Camels and unwashed dentures, I decide I'm moving in with Pete as soon as possible.

CHAPTER NINETEEN

"Al, you're taking big risks," Tony says. "You can't be taking something from every job we do. The clocks, the panties, the knickknacks. I can't be doing jobs with some goddam trophy hunter."

I'm glad Mama's tucked away in the bedroom. She doesn't like knowing about the panties and such.

Tony paces back and forth across the living room. The muscles in his arms ripple and his jaw is tighter than a vise. Dad's sitting at the kitchen table sipping black coffee and smoking his Camel. He's not saying anything, but his eyes show amusement. Dad's hard hat is cocked back.

"Damn it, Al. I'm serious. I'm not doing any more jail time because of some old fart who can't stay professional from beginning to end."

Dad's eyes gloss over, brown blazes of primal anger. I shrink back into the plastic couch thinking that a fight is about to start. Tony's pushing Dad too far. I thought Tony knew him better.

"That's a lie, Tony. I am a professional. I haven't been in the joint since 1967 and I ain't gonna be going back."

Tony stops pacing and glares at Dad. The air in the room is rancid because of Dad's chain smoking and his body odor.

"I been doing what I'm doing before you was a pup. So don't you be telling lies about me. I've taught you things you never knew." Dad snuffs out his Camel and stands up, fists tightening at his side. "Do you want to settle this right now?"

"Don't start using that fighter's stance, Al. We both know you could mop the floor with me. You're stronger than any man I've ever known."

Dad's fists unclench. The blaze in his eyes flickers out and his grin is lopsided.

"All I'm saying, man, is we have a good thing going here and I don't want to mess it up. I'm telling you that trophy hunting takes on risks we don't need."

Dad sits back down, flicks his Zippo, and lights another cigarette.

Tony's a smart, cunning man. He and Dad have made some big scores. He also knows that Dad is as powerful as a weightlifter. Only last week Dad carried a 200-pound safe the length of five football fields to the getaway van. Yeah, Dad fools everyone, even the cops. He may look fifty-six with his deep-creased face, but he still has the body strength of a man thirty years younger. Working forty hours a week on road crews running heavy equipment, working as a bump boy and screed operator keeps him 'fit as a fiddle' as Mama says.

"Before we go out tonight, take a dip in the pond or something. You're smelling ripe and I have to sit in that van with you all the way to Fresno." Tony nods at me and leaves.

When the rustle of Tony's footsteps fade into the distance, Dad laughs out loud and says to me, "He looked like some bantam rooster ready to take over the farmyard. Helluva partner."

Mama comes in from the back room, grabs a glass of buttermilk, and sits by me on the sofa. I can tell her hips are paining her and her breathing is becoming more and more shallow. Mama looks all of her seventy odd years except for the natural darkness of her hair.

Dad begins taking Polaroids out of a shoe box. Some are pictures of houses he's robbed. Some are pictures of naked ladies and young girls. The first time I saw the porno pictures I couldn't figure out what they were, because he had taken shots of only their breasts and private places. No faces. No identifying features. No sign of life. He holds one of the snapshots in his hand and rubs his finger over and over the photo. It's almost as if he's caressing it.

The folds in his face relax and his eyes drift away. Sometimes, I think he's remembering every scene in every picture, in every robbery, in every sexual tryst. Tony's right. Dad is a trophy hunter. Does he think he becomes part of their lives when he takes out one of his Polaroid cameras or steals some personal item from them?

Besides his clocks, he has collections of girls' driver's licenses, school identification cards, and personal snapshots you might find in someone's wallet. I have found items of clothes like panties, hose, shoes, and dresses.

As soon as Dad and Tony leave for Fresno, I pack my suitcase, stuff in money I've been hiding, and grab my car keys. When I pass through the living room, Mama looks up with a question in her eyes.

"I'm leaving here, Mama. I'm fifteen years old. Older than you were when you got married. It's time." I run my fingers back through my hair pulling it from my face and stare at Mama.

Tears are watering in her eyes. She starts rocking back and forth, back and forth. I lean down and kiss her dampening cheek. I whisper a good-bye.

She grabs my arm. "Don't leave, baby. You're all I got."

"Can't stay here another minute. Not with Dad and all." I shift my eyes away wondering if all the pain and hate I'm holding in, and all the secrets are shining through like pictures on a television screen.

"So you're jus' leaving me here with him! I always thought what you didn't know couldn't hurt you. He's had me, too. Yes, me, with my fused hips and arthritis. Broke your Papa's heart. He drunk hisself to death tryin' to forget what happened to me and his Krissy. Worryin' bout you is probably what keeled him over! Now you're leavin' me jus' like Papa did. Only worse, 'cause you could stay."

Mama's nostrils flare with every word. I don't think she ever said so much at one time before. Still, I can't stay. Can't ask her what she meant. My mind won't hold any more pain or secrets.

"I'm done with the lot of you!" I say, rushing from the room and the trailer. I don't realize I'm crying until the oncoming headlights blur. I push down harder on the accelerator. Speed will take me away and Pete will make me forget.

After a few days at Pete's, I feel safer. One morning right after Pete leaves for work, I'm cleaning up the dinner dishes when the apartment door opens.

"Did you forget your keys again?" I say as I turn expecting to see Pete. Instead Dad's huge frame fills the doorway. His brown eyes blaze.

When he stops to lock the door, I frantically search for a weapon. I seize the handle of a skillet. Before I can turn around, my father's bulk pins me to the counter and his Camel-laced breath is hot on my neck.

"You think staying here with this pretty boy is gonna keep me away from you or keep you away from the life. You gotta another think coming."

Dad grabs my upper arm, twists the pan from my grip, and drags me across the small apartment to the unmade bed. He throws me over on my stomach and enters me. The pain seers like a branding iron. With every thrust, I wish I were dead. I wish he were dead.

After he finishes, he sets his face next to mine and says, "That's what you needed, girl. A good butt-banging. Next time I'll shove it up so far your hair'll stand up on your head."

I keep quiet knowing he means it and knowing he'd do it again in minutes, if I talk back. I learned long ago that he likes me to fight, he gets more fun from it, he says.

"If you don't wanna be poking up daisies, you best get yourself up, get on one of them tight tee shirts I like, and come with me. We got family business to do. Don't want you to get too rusty, now, do we?"

CHAPTER TWENTY

I hate hospitals. I stare at the pale green walls and hear the groaning of the old lady in the bed next to me. I smell her cancer even though the nurses have tried to mask the scent of decay with Lysol. People prod and poke at me, pretending they care. When they say they don't want to hurt me, but still gouge me with syringes filled with penicillin, I forget it is for my own good. All of them think I'm just some white trash whore anyway. Who else gets gonorrhea?

My stomach started cramping a few days ago. The cramping became so painful that I thought my insides might fall out. Then the vomiting started. My chest and stomach muscles still hurt from all the heaving I've done. When I started shivering from the cold, Pete piled on blankets to warm me. Still, it felt like I was packed under piercing ice crystals. For once, I wanted to see a doctor.

Maybe I hate Pete more than hospitals. He gave me the clap. Mama will say it's God's way of punishing me for sinning and abandoning her. Dad'll just say I shouldn't be messing outside the family.

During evening visiting hours, Pete shows up carrying a Big Gulp and a withered pink begonia. He sets both on my dinner tray. After moving a chair closer to my bed, he draws the curtain around us. When he reaches for my hand, I stuff my arm under the cotton blanket. I say nothing except with my eyes that are staring a hole right through him.

"I'm so sorry, baby cakes. So sorry. I didn't know. Honest. Forgive me?"

He leans forward to kiss me, and I turn my face to the side.

"Please, Sandy. You know how much I love you."

Finally, I look at him and see the tight set of his jaw and the hollow, lost look in his grey eyes. His hair is falling forward in its Pete-like way. I have an urge to push it back. I clutch the bed sheet with my hand. Can't make it too easy. He should grovel a bit more.

While he chatters about work, a cranky customer, and a mixed up parts shipment, I realize how innocent he is. Life's so easy for him. He goes to his normal job, races his car, and comes home to me who he thought was a virgin.

As he talks, I nod off, tired from all the medication, tired of thinking.

"Sandy, what the hell? What the hell?" Pete says to wake me up.

Groggy, I focus and see him looming over me. He's holding my chart in his hand.

"It says here, you're only sixteen years old! How come we just celebrated your nineteenth birthday the other day? What a fool I've been to believe you. What other things have you been lying about?"

I start to sit up. My mouth is so dry I can't get any words out even if I knew what to answer.

"Never mind. I don't want any jail bait for a girlfriend."

Pete tosses my chart onto the bed and stomps from the room. I hear a cough from my nosy roommate. I muffle my sobs into the hospital pillow.

Only hours before, the grim-faced resident had explained that I could be permanently damaged and not have kids. Now Pete's left me and I feel like shit warmed over. Happy sweet sixteen to me!

After the hospital stay, I have no place to go except home. Mama's fussing over me in bed. She tucks the quilt around me like I'm a four-year-old and she promises to make me fried bologna.

"I'm so glad my baby's come home. I been missin' your smilin' face." She's grinning like a Cheshire cat without the teeth.

"Right," I say thinking I wish I were with Pete. Maybe I can get him back, then I wouldn't have to be here listening to this prattle and having my dad sniffing around me every night.

While I'm eating my bologna, Tony walks in.

"How are you doing, Sandy? Sorry to hear you had to have your appendix out, but if it got you to come home, good has come from it."

Tony sits on the end of the bed. The double mattress fills up most of the small room. I nod. Appendix, sure, Tony, whatever you think.

"Granny's missed you something fierce. Guess that's why she adopted that scrawny turkey. Gerky the Turkey what a name. Even housebroke it!"

"Yeah, she even showed me how it catches flies for her." I can't help but smile remembering her holding the turkey by its legs and circling it around the room.

Tony shakes his head.

"Your dad is one tough old bird himself. The other night, we set off a damn alarm and had to high-tail it back across the field. Your dad fell down, twisted his ankle up behind his leg, and couldn't get himself up. He had me check his gun to make sure he had plenty of bullets and told me to take off. They won't take me alive, your dad said. Now get the loot and get the hell outta here." Tony takes a breath and sips some of his beer. "I left him there, holed up in the muddy pasture and took off. Six hours later, I get back to Al and park the van up next to him. He's got his leg straightened out by then and I give him a good pull to get him on his feet. When we get to the car, he says he's driving. By hell, he did, too, seven hours back here to Bend."

Tony has a real admiration for my dad. Wonder what he'd think if he knew he was the lowest of the prison scum, a child molester. As usual, I best keep this information to myself if I know what's good for me.

At supper time, I hear Dad's latest girfriend Gladys. Her hyena laugh screeches from the kitchen. She annoys the hell out of me, but she's sweet on Dad. She has a camper truck and has been going with Dad to his paving job sites. I wish he'd move in with her permanently.

"Hello, everybody," I say as I enter the living room. I'm wearing a sheer nightie and Gladys turns crimson, not from embarrassment, but because Dad is staring at the outline of my breasts.

"Sandy, go cover yourself up. Your Daddy's home." Mama's shocked.

I sit on the couch anyway. "He's seen it all before, Mama. After all, he is my daddy."

The vein on Gladys' forehead is throbbing so hard that I wonder if it'll burst. Mama grabs a tattered afghan and tosses it to me. Dad looks around the room at each of us, enjoying the game I'm playing.

"Come on, Al, let's go to my place for some good home cooking," Gladys says. Her buck teeth push forward with each word. Her over-permed hair is as tight as her squinting eyes.

"That's a good idea, Gladys," I say as I smile sweetly.

When they leave, Mama says, "You got the devil in ya girl comin' in here like the whore of Babylon."

"Gladys isn't any saint. She's learning the burgling trade from Dad and bringing her son into it, too."

"I declare, child. You're filled with vinegar tonight. Must be feelin' a sight better."

"Yes, Mama, I am. I'd feel even better if Gladys made Dad her fourth husband. Kinda a miracle she's outlived three husbands, don't you think?"

"Ain't none of my business. She's making my Al happy is all I know."

While Mama stacks some Oreos on a paper plate for me and pours me a cup of milk, I fantasize about Gladys outliving Dad. I wish it would happen-real soon.

I'm gonna push them together as much as I can. That's one good way of keeping Dad out of my bed. The more jobs he does with Tony and Gladys, the less I have to do, too. Sixteen would be a good year to retire from this hell.

CHAPTER TWENTY-ONE

What a sight! Mama's rocking with Tinker in her lap and Gerky's roosting on top of her chair. Tony and I are sitting at the kitchen table.

"Did you see the diamond that farmer was sporting at the restaurant this morning? Doesn't need to keep it either. Pay for a lot of shoes for my kids," Tony says. He talks more like Dad every day. As he drums his fingers on the Formica table top, I figure he's planning how to steal and fence the diamond ring. Like Dad, he wants something, he gets it.

"Where's Big Al?"

"Gladys and Dad took off for Yakima. It's Friday, Dad's favorite work-day. Besides, Mama sent him looking for a new television."

Tony's eyebrow went up like a question mark. When I told him that Gerky had knocked over a pitcher of water that shorted out the whole TV, we both started laughing so hard that tears were streaming down my face.

"Gerky the Turkey. Gerky the Turkey," Tony repeated over and over again which set us back to laughing. "Truth is stranger than fiction."

When I look to see if Mama's laughing with us, I notice she has stopped rocking and her face is pale. The newspaper has drifted from her lap to the floor. "You alright, Mama?"

"Just feelin' a bit peaked, child."

"Can I get you something? Some water? Do you need one of your pills?"

When I kneel next to Mama, Gerky gobbles and flutters to a corner. Mama's forehead feels clammy. "Need a quilt? Are you cold?"

"I'm fine, chile. Stop fussin'. I been thinkin' though some biscuits'n gravy would taste right good. Could ya go get me some, baby?"

"Okay and I'll pick up some Pepsi, too. Are you sure you'll be okay, Mama?" Droplets of sweat have formed on her upper lip.

"Yeah, baby. Tony's here. Gimme a big kiss now before you head out. I love you, honey girl."

"Geez, Mama, I'm only going to the store." Still, I give her a hug and a wet kiss. She smiles up at me.

"Get on with ya, now." Mama flutters her hand through the air in her begone-with-you gesture.

When I return, I am greeted with the flashing lights of a squad car and rescue unit. Nothing starts the adrenalin flowing like fear. My hands slip on the steering wheel and I almost hit the squad car broadside. I run through the door, and a fireman is leaning over Mama. Tinker's yapping at him.

A policeman holds me back. "She's gone, Miss. I'm sorry."

Tony comes up from behind and hugs me close. I want to scream. Instead, I bury my face on Tony's shoulder and let the sobs come.

That night Tony's sitting with me on the couch. I'm cuddled up in Mama's ragtag afghan. It still has the scent of her favorite rose toilet water.

"She knew she was dying, Sandy. That's why she sent you off. Didn't want to burden you."

"Just like her, not wanting to be a bother. Still I wish I had been here with her. She was my Mama after all."

My words sound hollow within the trailer walls. We've lived so many places, Mama and me. Yuba City, Dallas, Salem, and Bend. There's probably been more towns and more addresses, but my memory fails me. The only constant has been her rocker and the afghan I'm hugging.

"She died in my arms. She wasn't alone," Tony says.

"I'm so glad you were here. She loved you like a son. Maybe better." I saw the grief settled in his eyes and took his hand in mine.

"She called me over to her chair and said 'I want to tell you something. I'm dying and I'm not afraid.' She was one brave woman. Not one second of panic."

Tony tosses a newspaper over to me. "Granny said to give you this picture. Said you'd understand."

On the front page, there's picture of two white horses grazing next to a white picket fence. What did this mean? What was I supposed to understand? Swirls of darting words mixed with flashing scenes as if a movie was rewinding. White horses? Papa was in this scene. It was the night he lay dying in my lap. Mama said something about white horses and white fences being there when she went.

A shiver slithers down my spine. Mama knew she was dying when she saw the paper. I explain to Tony that Mama had the sight.

"She said she was born with a caul over her face. The veil means having special senses. Knowing things." Then why didn't she know that she had spawned evil when she let Al live?

Tony and I talk into the night. I tell him about Mama's being married at twelve to her first cousin. The death of her twin babies when she was thirteen. Uncle Paul's birth. Dad's premature birth caused from her husband's beating her.

"She said her Al was a mite of a thing, not more than a couple of pounds. She kept him in a shoe box, covered him with fresh-picked cotton, and fed him with an eyedropper."

I'm thinking, but don't say, she should have let him die. He's brought nothing but grief and evil to everything and everyone in his path. Mama would have scolded me for that and said something like all God's creatures deserve a chance. When Dad wasn't blaming her for how he turned out, she was blaming herself. You made me what I am, you and your crazy husbands, he'd say.

"She's had a hard life. She was probably happy to meet her maker," Tony says to fill the silence.

I nod thinking about her other two husbands, other three children, and the sorrow of Dad making his own half-sister pregnant. Tony doesn't need to know it all. Mama believed in secrets, too.

Tony helps me get Mama buried. My real mother and uncle come to say their good-byes. Dad hasn't come home from his trip with Gladys. Probably best we couldn't reach him.

The three of us talk about Mama's pets and laugh about Mama's latest fondness for the CB. None of us talk about Dad. None of us share secrets.

Two days after the funeral, I come home from visiting Pete at his store and recognize Gladys's van in the driveway. In the trailer, Dad is installing another TV.

"Got the old lady a nice, new TV here," he says before standing to admire the walnut cabinet. "Heavier than a bitch to carry, too. Where is she?"

"She died last Friday night, Dad. Heart failure."

"That's a fine how-do-you-do. I up and find this TV and haul it around and nobody tells me she's dead already a week." He's swaying back and forth, hands on his hips.

"Dad, we didn't know where you were. I called the construction site and they said you were gone for a few days."

"You should have gotten word out somehow."

"Should I have called a 'Smokey' to track you down? That would have been really interesting. On second thought, maybe I should have called the cops, then you wouldn't be here yelling at me!"

"Don't push your luck, honey."

His voice lowers and his eyes are empty, brown and vacant. I shudder like death is still in the room.

CHAPTER TWENTY-TWO

"What'll you have?" the waitress asks. She takes the pencil from behind her ear and flips open the green page of the order pad.

I order my usual burger, fries, and Pepsi. I wave to another waitress who is sweet on Dad. She pops by and asks about him. I tell her he's doing fine that he's up in Washington state on another road job. I don't tell her that he's with Gladys. Why ask for trouble?

"Who's the new girl?" I ask and nod toward the waitress who took my order and is joking with a customer at the counter.

"Oh, you must mean Sally. She's been here about a month. Usually works mornings. Nice kid. About your age, I would guess."

After Sally sets the plate and drink down, I thank her.

"You must be Big Al's daughter. Am I right?" She has one of those perky voices and too-quick smiles. Her roots are deep brown against a henna dye job. She's tall and Twiggy thin.

"Right." I drop it there. She makes me feel a bit edgy.

After I eat and sip the last bit of the Pepsi from the glass, I think about ordering the lemon meringue pie. No, better not, now that I've dumped Pete. I might be on the prowl again. Pete threatened to marry some other girl and I told him to go ahead.

"I've got a short break. Mind if I sit?" Sally says, easing into the booth across from me.

"Guess not," I answer a bit testily.

"Al thinks you and I should get together. Thinks we could make a good team, if you know what I mean?" Sally lowers her voice and her smile peters out.

"Not really," I say. I've always kept family business to myself. Besides, why should I trust this stranger?

"Look, I'll let Al fill you in. Hey, why should you trust me, huh? A perfect stranger." Sally says. "Oops, the manager's giving me the evil eye. See ya later!"

Two days later, Dad says, "Look, Sally has a way to get her hands on some sweet jewelry. She wants me to fence it. I say to myself, hey, Sandy's ready to go out on her own."

He keeps talking. I keep listening. I say no. He says yes. Then the adrenalin kicks in and I feel the excitement building. Just me, planning it, doing it. Maybe I can do this.

It's countdown time. Sally and I have passed by the house that we're going to rob. I was surprised to learn that I know the woman who lives there. Marsha and I have chatted in line at the grocery store and at the gas pump.

I stake everything out like Dad taught me. On the downside, it's a two-story house, but there's good coverage from the bushes and a stand of aspens. The neighbors are far enough away that they shouldn't be a threat.

"Okay, you go to Marsha's party. Don't think she should see us together. You check out the master bedroom sometime during the evening. I'll give you some tape to keep the front door from locking. Then we wait," I say. This is feeling good. I have a workable plan.

Down the block from the party, I wait for Sally. The car's nose is facing Marsha's street and I can see everyone coming and going. It's midnight and people are starting to leave. Minutes later, Sally taps on the passenger window and I unlock her door.

"Did you circle around like I told you?"

"Yes, Sandy. Heck of a walk, too, especially at midnight."

An hour passes and stragglers have been leaving. The front porch lights turn off. Seconds later, a Lincoln backs out of the driveway.

"See I told you. Marsha and her husband always go out to breakfast afterwards. Let's move out." The eagerness in Sally's voice makes me nervous. She sees this as a game.

"Move out? Do you think we're a wagon train? Well, hold your horses. We're doing this my way. Now put on your gloves. I'm going straight to the master bedroom and you're standing guard. Got that?"

"Yeah, yeah, I got it. Let's do it!"

I warn Sally once more that she's staying put by the front door. She nods.

The door has scrolls and designs in the wood. It opens into the foyer and I take Sally by the shoulders and stand her by the side window. Before going upstairs, I trace the route to the backdoor.

The staircase carpet is so thick that a team of baseball players wearing their cleats wouldn't be heard. The bedroom is laid out just like Sally told me. I remove a pillow case and proceed to the open jewelry box. Then, I scour the other drawers quickly, finding a few more velvet jewelry boxes hidden with the lingerie. In the closet, I find a floral satin hosiery bag filled with hose and two ring boxes.

Cash is stuffed under scarves in the dresser and between the pages of a dusty family Bible. Marsha and her husband smile at me from an ornate, filigreed picture frame. The backing is thicker than it should be. Several hundred dollar bills are hidden between the cardboard and the photograph.

I survey the room carefully, fluff the pillow up beneath the bedspread, and close the lid to the jewelry box. Very professional, I say to myself. I open my coat and tie the pillowcase around my belt. The coat's bulk camouflages everything.

At the base of the stairs, no Sally. I call out softly. She comes bounding like an untrained Labrador.

"Look at this, Sandy. Must be jade, don't you think? Real jade."

My irritation mounts.

"I told you to stand guard. Let's get out of here. Now."

"There's more pieces in the dining room, too. Don't be such a spoilsport."

I ease over to the dining window and look to the driveway. No Lincoln. When I return to the front door, I turn. No Sally.

"I'm leaving with or without you, Sally." I open the door cautiously. Sally appears out of the darkness and slips through ahead of me. After stripping the tape from the lock, I quietly close the door. We follow the shrubs around to the neighbor's front yard and enter the street. No traffic. No dogs barking.

My heart pounds so loud all the way back to the car, I wonder if Sally can hear it. For once, she is quiet.

We ease away from the curb and travel away from Marsha's house. Sally wants to celebrate. I tell her she's crazy. Al has waited for us at the trailer. He sizes up each piece. Tells Sally he should be getting fifty cents on the dollar for the stuff. She pouts.

"This is good stuff. We should get a lot more."

"That's the rate, take it or leave it."

"Can you pay me now?"

"Hell, no, do I look like a bank? I'll get in touch next weekend. Rest your heels for a while and keep your mouth shut."

"Now where were you tonight?" I ask Sally.

"Went home straight after the party. Left my clock radio set to go off, soft-like at one o'clock. The old crone next door will hear it. The walls are paper thin."

"Good," I say. "I'll call you as soon as Al makes the deal."

Dad follows Sally out the door. Gladys has been waiting in the truck for him. She's probably as happy to see the jewelry as Sally was.

Sally didn't bring out the jade figure she had palmed and I didn't say anything. The roll of bills I had pocketed would tide me over for quite a

while. Nobody knew about the cash and nobody would. I wouldn't owe
Dad any more favors.

On Monday Sally calls me. She sounds out of breath and like she's
whispering in a roomful of people. "Sandy, the police just came by the
restaurant to talk to me. I almost peed my pants."

"Why would the police stop by to see you?"

"You know why, you idiot. Marsha gave them the names of everyone
at her party."

"So. You didn't do it, did you?"

"Are you nuts or something? What am I going to do?"

"First of all, calm down and stop calling me names. I'm not an idiot
and I'm not nuts. Just tell the police the truth. That's the best way. What
did you do after the party?"

Sally hangs up on me.

Hours later, a squad car drives up our lane. I am sweeping the kitchen
floor when the officer pokes his head through the open door.

"Miss, could I talk to you?" he asks.

"Whatever for? Come on in."

He holds his cap and twists it in circles. His eyes shift around the
room. Other than Dad's collection of clocks everything appears normal.
After Mama died, I shoveled out her piles of magazines and trash. I
washed the whole place down and was pleased that the trailer cleaned
up so well.

"Do you know a Sally Glantz?"

"I'm not sure. How should I know her?"

"She's a waitress at the City Cafe. She says she knows you."

"Oh, that Sally. Sure I know her. Just didn't know her last name. Was
she in an accident or something?"

"Not exactly."

He told me she had been arrested for burglarizing a woman's house.

"You're kidding? She doesn't look the type."

"She says you were with her."

"What!" My face starts burning and my heart pounds like thunder.

"Come down to the station with me and we'll clear this right up."

The nightmare is real. I close the door behind me, forgetting to lock it, forgetting everything except the pounding in my ears. The officer says he has to put me in the back seat. The wire mesh divider brings back all the memories of my trips to Salem Prison. Was I headed for a cage? Would I be one of the young bloods targeted for sex by some bull dyke?

Sweat pours between my breasts and shoulder blades. I hug myself as we drive. Oh, God, I miss Mama. Desperately, I start thinking of Dad and what he would do. In my head, I keep saying innocent until proven guilty, over and over again.

Two men come at me with question after question. I'm scared. Who wouldn't be? I was with my dad and his girlfriend that night. We had dinner and a few beers then they left for Washington. Why Washington state? Because my dad works with a road crew up there. He'll be back this weekend, I say. No, I can't reach him. He might call me though. Usually does midweek, I tell them.

The light is so bright I feel like my eyes will be sunburned before they finish with me. There's a mirror on one wall. Probably someone watching me. I'd die for a Pepsi.

"We'll be back," one says. "Gonna check some facts."

I put my head on the table to shield myself from the lights and the peering glances of anyone on the other side of the glass. I need a bathroom, but I don't want to ask.

An hour later they return. One hands me a glass of water.

"We've got a little problem. Sally says you burgled the house. She says you planned it all and did the job. All she did was to unlock the door for you."

"She must be nuts! I don't know her. I don't rob people. This is crazy!"

No one says anything for a minute. Dad says they use silence to make you uncomfortable so you start talking. I sit and let the tears fall down my cheeks.

"Can I go home now?" I say. "Can I have a Kleenex, please?"

I sniff loudly and pathetically. It's not too hard to cry since I am scared spitless.

One guy hands me a box of Kleenex. I wipe at my eyes and drink a sip of water.

"We could clear this all up," the other man says.

"How?"

"Lie detector test." He sits on the edge of the table, a friendly smile on his face. "What do you say?"

Dad has told me that he's faked the machine plenty of times. Says all I have to do is tighten my butt muscles like steel whenever I'm about to lie. I don't know if it's true or not. If it's not, my goose would be cooked.

"I guess so. Am I under arrest or something?"

They read me my rights.

"But I didn't do it," I say.

"The lie detector test is the ticket then. If you pass that, we send you home."

"Could you read me those rights again to make sure I understand?" I know them by heart since Dad has a ditty he sings about them.

He reads them again.

"So I can have a lawyer, is that what you said?"

"Yeah."

"And make a phone call?"

The heavyset detective nods.

"Maybe I should do that before I take the test."

You could see the flash of anger between the two detectives. They shut the door loudly when they leave the interrogation room.

Tony sends a lawyer he knows, a man named McIntyre. The lawyer raises hell when he arrives at the station house. You mean you questioned her without reading her rights first? She is a minor. She may look twenty-one to you, but she's only seventeen. Are you charging her or not? No lie detector test. No way.

Mr. McIntyre drove me home in his burgundy-colored Cadillac. He has sharp features, a bulging belly, and a fringe of gray hair around his bald head. He reminds me of a younger version of Papa. He grills me about everything that had happened from when the officer came to the house and when the detectives started questioning me. He never asks me if I did steal the lady's jewelry.

When I get out of the car, he says, "You be really careful. You hear me. Don't say anything to anyone. Don't trust a living, breathing soul except for me."

"Thank you, Mr. McIntyre."

"Don't thank me yet, little lady. This isn't over, not by a long shot."

I jump every time the phone rings. When a car drives anywhere near the trailer, a chill runs through me. All I can think of are cages, bodies buried in walls, and body parts shoved down drain pipes. With sleep comes nightmares, with daylight comes daymares.

Sally calls three times. Every time, I tell her she is looney tunes and hang up on her. Maybe the phone is tapped or she is calling from the police station with the cops listening. In the past, the FBI has tapped our phones, and once tried to put a hidden microphone in Dad's jacket pocket. Dad took great pleasure in setting the receiver by a blaring radio for hours before flushing the device down the toilet.

I go into town for some groceries and Tampax. I always start my period when I'm under stress. This is way beyond stress.

After a quick shopping trip, when I drive up to my place, Sally is sitting on my front stoop.

"What are you doing here?" I ask. "Haven't you caused me enough trouble?"

"I'm sorry really I am, Sandy."

"Look, lady. You're a fruitcake. Get off my steps and out of my yard or I'll call the cops on you." I push her to the side and struggle to get my key in the door. I don't want her to see my hand shaking.

I twist the knob, set the groceries inside the door, and turn to face Sally. Her eyes are puffy from crying and red blotches cover both cheeks. She's a worse mess than I am.

"Leave. Now."

"Does your dad have my money yet? I need it for a lawyer." She's almost on her knees begging me. If she hadn't ratted me out, I might feel sorry for her. As it is, I have to get her out of my yard and out of my life.

"You really are nuts." I say and slam the door in her face.

She starts pounding on it and I can feel the vibrations on my back. "You really are a bitch!" she shouts. Finally, there is silence.

The next morning Mr. McIntyre calls me and says to get down to his office. Fear pounds in my chest all the way downtown. I drive like a madwoman.

His secretary leads me through a brass-trimmed door into his office. He's on the phone with someone. I sink down into a red leather chair. Wood paneling and an Oriental rug give the office a feeling of luxury. Some of the houses I've burgled smell like this, leather and wood…and money.

"They're not going to prosecute," he says. "Not you anyway. Sally was caught with some of the stolen items, two jade figures."

My stomach unknots and my lungs allow themselves to fill with air.

"Then it's over?"

"For now, at least. If Sally goes to trial, you may be called to testify or you might be requestioned about her. Call me immediately."

"Thank you, Mr. McIntyre. Thank you so much."

"If you're lucky, they'll offer her a plea and you won't be involved. That's probably what will happen. Let's hope so. As for you," he hesitates.

I draw in a breath.

"You're closing in on eighteen. It won't go easy if you're picked up then. Do you understand me, young lady?"

CHAPTER TWENTY-THREE

Bend, Oregon, 1978

"Tony says you beat the rap. Congratulations, honey. You're a chip off the old block," Dad says patting me and himself on the back.

"Thank goodness, Sally plea-bargained. That chapter in my life is closed for good."

Even though the trailer has heated up like an oven in the October sun, Dad still wants his coffee. I set the mug in front of him and start to sit down. He latches onto my arm.

"Let's do a little real celebrating. I gotta a job for us over in Salem. You want to get back in the saddle so you don't lose your edge."

I yank my arm away. "Not me, Dad. Count me out. It's over."

"Nothing's over till I say it's over," Dad says. His voice is colder than an Oregon winter.

"Where's Gladys?" I figure changing the subject will buy me a little time.

"She's out with her grandkids. That Maybelle is a cutie, that's for certain."

Won't he ever stop? I thought men started slowing down when they reached middle age. I'd like to hang him by his balls, or better yet, stuff them down his throat.

"I see that wild look in your eye, honey. Jealous of little Maybelle? Don't you know you're my favorite girl?"

If he knew what I was really thinking, he'd probably bury me in the Deschutes River Woods along with those other girls. They were too young to die. So am I.

"Come on over here, honey. Give me some sugar."

"Daddy, I'm not your honey and I don't want to give you anything right now."

"Didn't I just tell you that nothing's over till I say it's over?"

With those words, he reaches across the table and wrenches my arm so tight I think it will snap. I try to tug my arm away, but he holds it tighter as he lifts me out of my chair. I kick at his shins. He laughs and twists my arm behind my back.

On the bed, he yanks off my jeans. Then he shreds my panties. He ties them around my neck and twists them into a tight knot. I gag and watch the glistening in his brown-black eyes.

"See how easy it is. I could kill you right here. Right now. I've done it before and I can do it again. Nobody ever says no to Big Al."

As he loosens his grip and the cloth falls away, I see the evil lurking in his eyes and the creases in his face. His thrusts are like a thousand daggers. If the mattress wasn't flat on the floor, the frame would have given way. When the brutality stops, he says, "Tall Timber missed you, honey."

He zips his pants and stands over me. The smile that curls up his big lips makes my skin crawl.

"I hate you! You smelly old man! I hate you! Don't you ever come near me again! I'll kill you, do you hear me? I'll kill you."

"Whatever, honey."

His calmness makes me even angrier. That's when I realize that in my tirade, I found the way out. The only way out.

The next night I call the police. I tell them someone is prowling around the yard. They come out, check around, and promise to cruise by a few times during the night.

Tony drops by the next morning.

"Why were the cops here last night?" He's anxious as a tiger in a cage.

"I saw someone walking out back last night. Scared me."

"I didn't see anyone, but I'll keep my eyes peeled. Maybe you should get a dog now that Tinker passed on."

Tony had helped me bury Tinker under a bush in the back acre. I think Tinker died from loneliness when Mama passed on.

"A dog is a lot of trouble, Tony. Besides, I probably won't see anyone lurking around again."

"I get nervous with you here by yourself since your dad is in Washington on that road crew. Maybe you should go stay with him and Gladys for a while."

Right, I think to myself. One big happy family. If Tony knew the truth, he'd probably wring Dad's neck.

"Hey, it was probably my imagination. Alone and all."

My loneliness comes in waves as I think of Mama. If I forget to turn off the CB radio, a trucker's voice eerily calls Mama's handle, Granny-in-the-woods. A smile comes before the tears start.

Two nights later, I call the police again. The officer acts a little irritated at first. Then I ask him if Sally is out of jail and lie about how she threatened me. He says he'll check it out and someone will call me back.

"Meanwhile," he says, "I'll make some extra turns by your place tonight."

A policeman does call and assures me that Sally is still in jail.

"Now, there has been a peeper spotted a few times around your area. Maybe it's him trying to get an eyeful," he says. "Call us again if you see anything unusual."

A peeper, I say to myself. Is Dad working this route again? That brings a smile to my face.

I call Tony and tell him about the neighborhood peeper.

"Do you think I'm safe?" I ask.

"Most peepers just look, but I've heard that a few rapists start peeping first. Guess when it's not a thrill anymore, they move up the excitement ladder."

Tony shows up after supper to check on me. I assure him that I'm fine.

"Do you have a gun?" he asks.

"You know I hate guns, Tony. I'm scared I'll shoot myself."

"How about a shotgun? It's hard to kill yourself with one unless you put it in your mouth. Even then, it's tough to reach the trigger."

Tony brings me a shotgun the next morning. He shows me how to load it. Then we practice target shooting in the backyard. The action jars me so bad, I think my shoulder will be bruised for a month.

"Even if you don't hit the pervert, you'll scare him to death," he says. "I sure as hell hate perverts. Scum. That's what they are."

"I don't understand them at all," I say.

"What's to understand? Perverts, rapists, and killers are hopeless psychopaths. They should all be shipped to Devil's Island," Tony says.

When Tony starts talking about his psychology theories, he gets long-winded. He says policeman as a whole are so stupid. They pigeonhole criminals and come up with ridiculous profiles.

"Nobody catches someone with a profile," Tony says. "It's hard work and street smarts. When I was a cop, I could smell a criminal. I could get in his head and make him come to me. Take your dad, for instance. Because he's old and worn looking, people underestimate him. He's the strongest man I know. He could toss me over his shoulder, snap my neck, and hurl me across the room without getting winded. Because he's been caught for robbing in the past, that's all they think he does. Pigeonholing works out great for your dad. He could get away with murder."

When Dad's clocks chime ten o'clock, Tony finishes his coffee.

"Promised the missus that I'd be home early tonight. You be careful now, you hear. Don't forget to use that shotgun if you need to."

Three nights later Dad calls.

"I'll be dropping by in a few minutes. You be ready for your daddy, you hear?"

Rain hits the trailer roof and wind whips a tree limb into the aluminum walls. Muted light shines through the louvered window. The loaded twelve-gauge lays on the floor next to Mama's rocker. I pick it up and set the barrel across my lap. I caress it like it's a newborn.

Tires disturb the gravel in front of the trailer. I stand and brace myself against the living room wall. Heavy footsteps sound on the path and the trailer steps. Dad tries the lock. I hear keys jangling. I hear him muttering as he tries to fit his old key in the new deadbolt. I hear him walk away, a truck door slams, and again footsteps. He'll pop the door open with his trusty screwdriver. Perfect, I think, as I raise the shotgun.

There's a grinding snap and the door pops open. I close my eyes and fire.

A thunderous roar shatters the night as I'm thrust backward into the wall. When I open my eyes, a hole, the size of a man's fist has shattered the roof-line over the door.

"I'll be a sonuva bitch," Dad says.

"That you are, Dad. That you are."

EPILOGUE

In spite of the years of sexual abuse, emotional depravation, and betrayal, I have survived. I am thankful that I did not succeed in killing my father or I, too, would have been lost. My botched attempt at murder did end the sexual abuse. Although my father's widespread, ongoing criminal activities continued unpunished, I was no longer his accomplice.

Through the years, unanswered questions have accumulated about my father. I have collected records from local, state, and federal governments. They only created more questions. The extent of his crimes remains a mystery, but I do know that he was a violent man with the ability to destroy lives and had the power to coerce others to do his bidding.

My father died in 1989. He outsmarted the police, but he could not control his cancer, heart condition, or the hand of God.

My healing happened slowly over time. I finally realized that anger was eating me alive and I was wasting all that anger on someone who had no remorse. To stop being a victim, I had to let go of the hatred and put it behind me.

ABOUT THE AUTHOR

Sandy Wilson shares her childhood experiences so that others may have a better understanding of sexual abuse and child exploitation.

Writer, S. Bolton's articles, short stories, and essays have appeared in anthologies and both regional and national publications. As a ghost-writer, she has published titles on sexual harassment and sales management.

Printed in the United States
140196LV00006B/29/A